Traveler's Guide to the Firearm Laws of the Fifty States

Twenty-fifth Edition -- January, 2021

AF722920

"Serving America's Gun Owners since 19

The following changes in state firearm laws were enacted by the various state legislatures during the 2020 calendar year. These changes, along with updates to the reciprocity, contact information & traveler's checklist coverage constitute the primary differences between the 24th and 25th editions. Owners of past editions should also be aware that most state pages have been revised over the last five editions to provide more in-depth information in an easier to understand format.

California: 9th Circuit rules state magazine ban goes too far – California seeks full court review
Colorado: Colorado Supreme Court affirms constitutionality of Colorado's magazine ban
Hawaii: residents moving guns out-of-state must notify county within 5 days if move is permanent
Idaho: permitless carry extended to any U.S. citizen
Illinois: Idaho & Nevada residents may apply for Illinois permits
Indiana: Attorney General opinion confirms that localities may not infringe upon gun rights
Iowa: range protection and strengthened preemption law
Louisiana: permittees allowed carry in churches w/limitations; preemption law enhanced, no local regulation in public buildings or commercial establishments
Michigan: Attorney General says Capitol commission may ban gun carry at the State Capitol
Missouri: St. Louis enacts illegal ordinance banning gun carry in city parks
Montana: Referendum 130 passed, localities now prohibited from restricting firearms carry in all areas except publicly-owned buildings
New Mexico: Albuquerque begins to enforce illegal carry bans within city limits
South Dakota: a loaded firearm may be carried in a snowmobile or an ATV w/o a permit
Virginia: preemption law weakened, localities may prohibit carry in many public areas; red flag law enacted; bump stocks banned.
Washington: carry prohibited in most childcare centers
West Virginia: preemption law strengthened, no local carry bans at fairs & festivals
RV "Boondocking": new section in "Traveler's Checklist" detailing each state's rules regarding RV carry while "boondocking" in parking lots and other related areas
Reciprocity: availability of updates at www.gunlawguide.com for conditional reciprocity states

Traveler's Guide
P.O. Box 2156
Covington, KY 41012
(859) 491-6400

www.gunlawguide.com

Peter J Cesnakas & Associates

How to Use this Guide

Firearm laws can be quite intimidating when traveling outside one's own state. Many horror stories exist in which the nonresident traveler is arrested on a felony charge for a violation that wouldn't qualify as a misdemeanor in the traveler's home state. A routine traffic stop suddenly degenerates into a nightmare journey through the criminal justice system. The unsuspecting traveler is hauled off to jail and forced to await the intervention of an attorney while his vehicle is searched and later impounded.

One story typifying this situation occurred several years ago on the New Jersey turnpike. A businessman from North Carolina was traveling to Maine via New Jersey when he was stopped by a New Jersey State trooper for a speeding violation. During the routine questioning, the trooper asked the North Carolina man if he had any firearms in the vehicle. Having a concealed carry permit from North Carolina, the traveler assumed he was operating well within the law. He told the trooper that he had a Glock 19 semi-automatic pistol in his briefcase that he was licensed to carry and would be more than happy to allow the trooper to inspect it. Before the traveler could utter another word, the trooper had drawn his sidearm, pointed it at the traveler and began shouting at the man to exit the vehicle at once with his hands in the air. The stunned businessman, who had never had so much as a parking ticket, did as the officer demanded. He soon found himself spread eagle on the ground while the agitated trooper called for assistance. In the days after his arrest, the traveler was charged with a felony and spent three days in a Newark jail. He was eventually placed in a diversion program while the felony charge was pled down to a misdemeanor. But if the traveler had not possessed such an exemplary prior record, he may have faced the original felony and prison time. In traveling through New Jersey, the traveler failed to take into account the radical difference in legal firearms carry from his native state of North Carolina. Such a lapse could have cost him much more than it did.

This guide will prevent such an incident by providing an outline of the legal pitfalls a traveler may encounter while carrying his firearms from state to state. Beginning with Alabama and continuing in alphabetical order through Wyoming, each state is afforded one page of explanation pertaining to the firearm laws most relevant to the traveler. The District of Columbia, Canada and Mexico are also covered. A bar graph showing how each state is rated for its treatment of firearms is displayed in the top margin of each page. Any change in firearms freedom from the previous year is noted by a (+) or (-) as well as the reason behind the change. When no change has occurred, the author provides the reader with a short phrase summarizing why the state has its current rating. This provides a quick reference when time is of the essence. Vehicle carry, concealed carry and reciprocity for non-resident licensees, and laws governing possession of all firearm types are covered in a user-friendly format for each state.

Shall Issue vs. May Issue

The reader will find the terms "shall issue" and "may issue" used extensively throughout this Guide. "Shall issue" refers to the statutory language in states where the issuance of a license to carry concealed is not dependent upon the discretion of a local law enforcement officer. If an applicant satisfies a number of objective criteria (ie. no felony record, no record of mental defect, etc.) and completes whatever training course is mandated by the law, the applicant ***must*** be issued a license regardless of what the issuing authority personally thinks of the individual. Most states with concealed carry laws operate their licensing procedure in this manner.

"May issue" refers to states that allow a certain amount of discretion over the issuance of a permit to carry a firearm. The local sheriff may require that the applicant demonstrate a viable need to carry a weapon by showing that the applicant has had his life threatened recently or requires a gun because of his current occupation. Fortunately for gun owners, "may issue" states are rapidly becoming an endangered minority. The recent flurry of interest in concealed carry laws has forced most states that formerly had discretionary issuance to amend their laws to make them "shall issue."

Reciprocity and Recognition

The traveler's concern with the concealed carry law of the various states is rooted in the issue of reciprocity. Many states with concealed carry licensing laws will recognize the out-of-state carry permits of travelers under certain conditions. Some of these states provide universal or "automatic" recognition for any foreign state's permits. These states will recognize any valid, out-of-state permit to carry a firearm regardless of bureaucratic interpretation. Other states will qualify their recognition of a foreign state's permits on the foreign state recognizing the permits of the host state or having issuance standards which are similar to the standards of the host state. Recognition of permits in these states is often at the discretion of the attorney general or state police. Such discretion indicates the potential for inconsistency. Travelers journeying to these states should verify the status of their out-of-state permits if they intend to use their permits for firearms carry. An up-to-date list is provided on p. 65 with the reciprocity status of the conditional states at the time of printing. Travelers may also further confirm the status of the states they are visiting by contacting any one of the official state agencies listed on p. 63 or by viewing updates to this list at www.gunlawguide.com. Some states modify their reciprocity lists without warning. So verification is always a good idea. Readers of the print version may use the map (p.10) to color code the states where their permits are recognized.

An issue that is fast becoming a problem for travelers is that of non-resident permits. More and more states are issuing permits to persons who are not residents of the issuing state. And some states that do not issue permits to nonresidents will make special exception for military personnel stationed in the state. This has been of immense benefit to citizens living in restrictive states such as New Jersey who sometimes find it almost impossible to acquire in-state permits. But the downside has been a number of states that are refusing to recognize out-of-state permits that are issued to persons who are not residents of the issuing state. Various reasons are given as to why this is being done. None of these explanations really answer the question as to why a non-resident, who passes through the same background checks as a resident, is less qualified for recognition than a resident. The bottom line for the traveler is that this can be a sticky wicket. When checking the recognition status of your permit, be sure to note which states do not honor non-resident permits. These states are set apart on p.65-67 with a star (*). States that do not recognize out-of-state permits held by their own residents are <u>underlined</u> on those same pages.

When carrying concealed outside of one's vehicle in a state that provides reciprocity, the traveler carries subject to the restrictions imposed on concealed carry in that state. Most states only issue licenses for handgun carry. States that allow other weapons to be carried are covered in the Traveler's Checklist. So travelers should be aware of which weapons may be carried with a permit before carrying anything other than a handgun. Persons should also have immediate possession of their carry permits and watch for postings that prohibit carry in certain areas such as public parks and government buildings. If approached by a police officer for a law enforcement purpose, the permittee should notify the officer that he has a carry permit with a concealed weapon. This action may not be legally required in all states. But it will help to immediately establish one's status as a law-abiding citizen.

Concealed vs. Plain View

The meaning of "concealed vs. plain view" might vary from state to state depending on how the statutes and case law of a particular state define them. Generally, however, concealed includes readily accessible firearms that are "hidden from ordinary observation on or about one's person." While in a vehicle, this definition would almost always include under one's outer clothing or in a closed container such as a purse or gym bag that is actually carried by the person. Many states also regard having a hidden firearm within arms reach to be carrying concealed. This would include glove compartment, console box and seat pocket containment.

Plain view usually refers to firearms that are visible from a vantagepoint outside the vehicle. This carry mode is utilized primarily while the vehicle is occupied and the owner wishes to have immediate access to his firearms for personal defense. In a holster or sling while on the vehicle's dashboard, passenger's seat or gun rack is considered acceptable in most states that mandate plain view carry. Travelers carrying firearms in plain view may find it prudent to secure their weapons in a trunk or rear storage area when they are not occupying the vehicle. All states which allow plain view passenger compartment carry allow cased and unloaded trunk transport as well.

Important Terms Defined

In the "Travelers Checklist," the subheading ***"standard firearms & ammo"*** refers to the possession or sale of "non-military pattern" handguns & long guns as well as commercially available ammunition common to most firearms. Some states will not permit mere ownership of these items without a permit and may go as far as to require a license to simply possess them in your own home. If a state requires a license, that detail is noted. Also, any relevant restrictions affecting the traveler are mentioned. But restrictions affecting items uncommon to the travelers (ie. flechette rounds, armor-piercing steel core ammo, exploding rounds, etc.) are not covered.

*"**Semi-auto & high capacity magazines**"* refers to military-pattern weapons and magazines capable of holding more than 10 rounds of ammo. Some states will prohibit certain semi-automatics based solely on their appearance. And those same states may also ban magazines over 10 shots.

"Machine guns & suppressors" refers to such items as are owned under the relevant portions of the National Firearms Act. "Bump Stocks" are devices that simulate full-auto fire on semi-autos and are prohibited in all states by a 2019 federal ruling by BATF.

The section entitled ***"Vehicle Carry for non-permittees"*** refers to vehicle carry by persons *without* recognized permits. Most states allow persons with recognized permits to carry handguns anywhere in the vehicle. Specific exceptions are noted in the text. Those persons who do not have permits must follow certain statutory rules for vehicle carry. This section examines these rules.

The term ***posted*** is used repeatedly in the text and simply refers to businesses or other entities that may post signs prohibiting firearms carry on their premises.

The terms ***permittee*** and ***non-permittee*** are used throughout the Guide. A permittee is a person who possesses a carry permit that is recognized in the state being discussed. A non-permittee is a person who does not possess a recognized permit in that state. Unless otherwise noted, these terms only include *non-enhanced* permits. *Enhanced* permits are only covered by specific reference.

Securely encased refers to firearms that are in closed commercial gun cases which are latched, but not necessarily locked, in place. "Securely encased" does not include firearms in cases not designed to hold guns. Purses, gym bags and briefcases do not qualify as securely encased containers. But hard plastic cases manufactured specifically for gun transport would be legitimate.

Constitutional Carry refers to states that allow some form of "on foot" concealed carry without a permit. These "permitless carry" states may provide an almost universal allowance for the right or may limit it to residents or to certain areas (ie. areas outside cities or towns).

Weapons allowed for licensed carry covers which weapons a particular state allows a person to carry under the authority of his permit. Most states limit this category to handguns only. But some states, such as Kentucky, allow any lawful deadly weapon.

State Parks is a section that covers the issue of carry by recognized permittees. Many states have carved out exceptions to general gun prohibitions for licensees but still prohibit open carry by non-licensees. As a rule, if a state allows concealed carry by permittees, it will also allow non-permittees to keep their firearms cased and unloaded in their vehicles. Many states may also allow handgun carry by permittees but will require long guns carried by anyone to be unloaded and cased.

Restaurants serving alcohol is a section limited to specific parameters for permittees. Restaurants are eating establishments such as Applebees or Fridays that serve alcohol but produce most of their income from the sale of food. The term would not include "Joe's Corner Bar" that may serve pizzas and pretzels but is primarily a "watering hole" for those wishing to imbibe. If the Guide indicates that permittees may carry in restaurants it means that permittees can carry concealed, loaded handguns if they do not consume alcohol, remain in the dining area and do not frequent the "bar portion" of the establishment. Granted, some states may allow permittees to drink and visit the bars of these restaurants, but enough states limit this privilege to make these guidelines necessary. Most states that allow carry in these restaurants allow businesses to post signs against such carry. Do not be surprised if you see some restaurants in "carry friendly" states posted against carry.

Duty to Notify LEO of permit status refers to the permit holder's duty to notify an approaching *Law Enforcement Officer* ***(LEO)*** that he has a concealed weapon and a license authorizing him to carry it. States will either require "immediate notification" upon initial contact with the officer or notification upon officer request. The states that require *immediate notification* put the burden on the licensee to tell the officer that he has a permit with a concealed weapon. Failure to immediately do so upon first contact can result in an arrest. So be especially careful in these states.

Right of Self-defense

The "Right of Self-defense" section in the Traveler's checklist indicates how each state protects a traveler's self-defense rights. It references whether a state has enacted an "NRA-model castle doctrine" in the last fifteen years and whether a citizen has a right to "stand his ground" in public areas and not retreat when threatened with deadly force. Most states have some form of the "common law castle doctrine" which provides *stand your ground* rights in your home. But many of the "NRA-model castle doctrines" extend this right to public areas outside one's home. Most reference any place "where a person has a right to be." Others limit the right to your vehicle. Some states may have "stand your ground" language in their case law but have not "codified" or "written it into" their statutes. These states are noted as being "not codified."

The section is not intended to provide the reader with in-depth knowledge of a state's self-defense laws. Rather it is meant to act as a barometer for the casual traveler in assessing a state's attitude toward self-defense rights outside of one's home. Too often, citizens who use deadly force to defend themselves are subsequently prosecuted by over-zealous district attorneys and even sued in civil court by their attackers. The result is a chilling effect. A citizen is afraid to use a gun for self-defense for fear of being turned into a criminal. This section will allow the traveler to determine which states are friendly to the citizen and which ones coddle the criminal.

Vehicle Gun Possession at Colleges

Most colleges and universities prohibit firearms carry in buildings and campus facilities. But some states have begun to carve out exceptions for gun possession in vehicles located on campus parking lots. The Guide provides an overview of this by classifying the regulatory action each state undertakes. Some states prohibit all gun possession on college campuses (vehicles included) through their criminal or administrative codes. Violating these rules could result in criminal sanctions such as arrest and prosecution. Other states allow each college to determine regulatory action through policy. Those connected in some way to the college (students, faculty and staff) are most at risk. They can be fired, expelled or face civil sanctions. Aside from muted trespass charges, not much can be done to penalize the occasional visitor. A small but growing number of states exempt those holding valid carry licenses from criminal action and, in some cases, also exempt all lawful gun owners. Perhaps the safest states are the ones such as Kentucky, which, along with exempting all gun owners from criminal sanctions, also prevent colleges from prohibiting vehicle gun possession through policy.

The Guide classifies each state based on these regulatory schemes. Readers should note that where vehicle gun possession is allowed, the firearm should remain locked in one's vehicle and hidden from view. If the state only exempts permittees, then only the weapons that one may carry with a valid permit (ie handguns) may be stored in the vehicle.

Some states exempt gun owners from criminal sanctions but allow the enforcement of college policy that could adversely affect those connected with the institution. These states are noted appropriately under each subheading. And readers should not be surprised to see "no gun" signs in campus parking lots where possession of lawful firearms is allowed. Some colleges still attempt to enforce "no gun" policies in spite of state laws that prevent such rules; proving that academics will often bend the rules to meet their own ideological ends.

Vehicle Gun Possession on K-12 School Grounds

Although most states prohibit gun possession within K-12 school buildings, some states have created exemptions for possession within vehicles located on school parking lots. The Guide covers this aspect in the Traveler's Checklist. But readers should be aware of several important parameters.

First, coverage is limited to permittees who are licensed by the state where the K-12 school is located. This is to be in conformance with both federal and state law. Federal law generally prohibits any loaded gun possession in or on school grounds or within 1,000 feet of such grounds. Firearms located on private property within the zone and guns possessed by persons licensed to carry by the state where the K-12 school is located may be loaded. So even though some states, such as Kentucky, do not require a license to have a loaded handgun in a vehicle, federal law would make any loaded gun possession illegal unless one had a license from the state where the school is located.

Second, coverage is generally limited to loaded handguns that are concealed from view and, when the vehicle is unoccupied, locked inside a secure compartment. Visible guns on school property are not recommended even if a specific state's law does not prohibit them. And most states restrict permittee carry to handguns only. So readers should assume the detailed exemption applies only to handguns and not to long guns whether loaded or unloaded.

And finally, this section is primarily intended to provide guidance for non-student adult parents who are attending some legitimate event on campus with a handgun in their vehicle. School employees may have separate policies for which they are responsible. While it would not be a criminal act for them to possess a gun in a vehicle in a state that allows such possession, they could run afoul of a personnel policy that could affect their future employment.

Loaded vs. Unloaded

The term "loaded" refers to firearms that have live ammunition in either the magazine or the chamber. A firearm with any number of rounds in its magazine is considered loaded under the laws of most states even if no live round is in the chamber. The four notable exceptions to this general rule are Colorado, Nevada, North Dakota and Utah which define "loaded" as only applying to firearms with a live round in the chamber. Some states consider guns that are in close proximity to magazines containing ammunition to be "loaded." Other states prohibit magazines from being inserted into firearms but allow loaded magazines to be located within arms reach of the firearm. These state-by-state differences are noted appropriately within the text.

Travelers should also keep all loaded firearms out of reach of their children while in a vehicle. A small number of states criminalize those who keep firearms in any place where a child might access the weapon. Some states, such as Ohio and Colorado, have specific laws in this regard. Other states may attempt enforcement through generalized laws involving child endangerment.

Open Carry

Carrying a handgun that is unconcealed on your person is a way for some persons to carry who do not have the benefit of a recognized permit. Many states do not criminalize such behavior; thus making this mode of carry legitimate under law. But travelers should use common sense when open carrying in populated urban areas where such carry is not widespread. Even in states that allow such carry in theory, police may stop and question an individual who is displaying a firearm on his hip for all to see. Granted, no person who is exercising a fundamental right should have to worry about being harassed for otherwise legal behavior. But such scrutiny can and does occur in the real world. A traveler should simply exercise good judgment and keep his handgun secured in a snapped, visible belt holster.

Interstate transport through restrictive states

Readers will also notice occasional references to the McClure-Volkmer Act of 1986 and its specific treatment of interstate firearms transport. This federal law is listed in the U.S. Code as an amendment to the Gun Control Act of 1968. It serves to correct certain draconian aspects of the 1968 law as well as make interstate transport of firearms less restrictive. Persons transporting firearms through a state that would otherwise view such transport as illegal may do so if the weapons are unloaded, cased and stowed in a trunk or vehicle storage compartment which is not readily accessible to the occupants. Any ammunition must also be kept separate from the firearms. Persons operating vehicles without trunks or external storage compartments may transport unloaded firearms in "locked" cases. Internal storage compartments other than console boxes or glove compartments that are locked may also suffice when a trunk is not available.

The traveler must simply be passing through the state and must be bound for a jurisdiction where possession of such weapons is legal. Any extended stops for reasons other than gas or emergency services would effectively nullify the traveler's interstate commerce classification and subject him to the effects of state law. For example, a traveler from Kentucky bound for Maine with Class III machine guns will pass through the state of New York. New York does not allow personal possession of machine guns. As long as the traveler maintains a steady, uninterrupted course through the state with the offending weapons stowed in the manner described above, he is operating within the parameters of federal law. As soon as the traveler stops to visit relatives in Albany, he falls within the police power of New York. He could be arrested for possessing firearms that are illegal under New York law. Some travelers have found it beneficial to have a hotel or campground pre-registration form with them when trekking through restrictive states such as New York. This form proves to any state trooper that you are actually traveling to a legitimate, gun-friendly destination and have no intention of remaining within the restrictive state for an extended period.

The Code only references firearms or ammunition. So the law *may* not cover a box of high capacity magazines (or other component parts) that are prohibited in a restrictive state. The courts have yet to "flesh out" the details of this aspect.

Traffic Stops

Any traveler carrying firearms should be aware of the proper way to handle a routine traffic stop. One involved in frequent travel will eventually be pulled over for a speeding violation or some other minor infraction. A motorist should avoid any erratic physical movements during a traffic stop. Both hands should remain on the steering wheel while the driver remains seated in the vehicle waiting for the officer to approach. At this point, the investigating officer has the right to ask questions of the motorist concerning his operation of the vehicle. Questions which may elicit self-incriminating information from the traveler may be refuted by simply informing the officer that the traveler would prefer to be represented by proper counsel before answering the posed question. Some officers may wish to go beyond mere questioning and conduct a search of the vehicle for contraband that could include firearms in some states. For an officer to conduct a legitimate search of a vehicle, he must have "probable cause." Most traffic stops do not provide the officer with enough probable cause for a search. Therefore, the officer will often politely ask the motorist for voluntary consent. Many citizens, fearing they will look guilty upon refusal, willingly sign the consent form the officer provides them. This is not a recommended course of action. Voluntary consent gives the officer free reign to do what he likes and nullifies any subsequent legal challenges. If asked to consent to a vehicle search, politely refuse and inform the officer that he will have to search on his own. Most officers who are unable to establish probable cause will not search without a consent form.

Travelers should note that a police officer might conduct a "protective search" of your person for weapons without probable cause. An officer may ask a motorist who appears suspicious to exit the vehicle so as to allow a frisk of the person's clothing for concealed weapons. The officer may also check the area of the vehicle under the motorist's immediate control for weapons before allowing him to reenter the vehicle. The courts allow this type of search only if the officer can articulate a reasonable suspicion that the motorist may have an illegal weapon. Such a protective search may not extend to other areas of the vehicle without probable cause of criminal activity.

Permittees sometimes wonder whether they should volunteer to an officer that they have a recognized permit if the officer does not ask. Most states do not require a citizen to divulge that information unless the officer requests it. But some states require the permittee to volunteer the information as soon as he is approached by a police officer. The states that require this action are noted in the text. As a general rule, it is recommended that no matter what the legal restriction, a recognized permittee should let an officer know that he has a permit with a gun on his person. Such notification will help avoid any escalation of what is already a tense situation. This notification is generally limited to permittees who carry under the authority of a permit. Firearms that are cased and unloaded in the trunk or storage area need not be declared unless a vehicle search is executed.

Also, recent reports indicate that police in anti-gun states such as Maryland are using license plate reader cameras to pull over gun owners from other states and search them for weapons. One family from Florida recently had their car emptied of all possessions, the husband handcuffed and the wife and kids searched because the Maryland trooper had information obtained from one of these cameras that the motorist had a carry license in his native state of Florida. The trooper claimed this gave him "probable cause" to harass the otherwise innocent family for almost two hours. Whether this is standard policy in Maryland has yet to be determined. But, be advised, this case illustrates how police in other states may know your license status before they even pull you over.

Universally Restricted Areas

Firearms carry is universally prohibited in certain areas even with a concealed carry permit. Federal installations such as Post Offices (including parking lots), courthouses and administrative offices and some federal management areas such as Corps of Engineers properties forbid gun carry inside buildings and, in most instances, on the outside premises. The Corps of Engineers enforces the "no guns" rule on any property it occupies, owns or leases to others. Many lakes formed by Corps of Engineers dam projects contain shoreline that is owned by the Corps. So travelers should be aware of Corps boundaries and carry firearms per McClure-Volkmer (p.5) when on Corps property.

Military bases prohibit firearms carry by visitors and also restrict firearm possession within one's vehicle. A recent Defense Department directive (5210.56) outlines gun possession policy on DOD property and also provides guidance as to how certain qualified personnel could be granted authority to carry personal firearms while on a military post. Visitors and military personnel should check with officials before visiting a military installation with firearms.

Most states prohibit firearms carry within preschool and primary & secondary school buildings (K-12). Harsh penalties are usually set for violating this restriction. And Federal law prohibits firearm possession within 1000 ft. of primary and secondary school properties. Concealed weapon permittees from the state in which the school is located, persons possessing unloaded firearms in locked containers inside their vehicles and private property areas within this zone are exempt from this prohibition. But someone carrying a loaded gun without a license within 1,000 feet of a school's property boundary would be in violation of federal law (although federal prosecutors have mostly used this as an "add-on" charge for drug and gang activity). Exceptions for vehicle possession by permittees on actual school grounds are covered separately on p. 4 of this section.

Firearms carry *may* also be prohibited in law enforcement offices, detention facilities, courthouses, most legislative meetings, some polling booths, many public buildings that house governmental offices where official business is conducted as well as mental health and day care facilities. Exceptions to these general rules do exist. But, for the most part, these areas are off-limits unless stated otherwise.

Retail establishments whose ***primary*** business is the sale of alcohol by the drink (bars) may have restrictions that vary from total prohibition to gun carry absent any alcohol consumption. Travelers should avoid carrying into these areas unless the specific rule for that state is known.

Hotels & Lodgings

Questions often arise as to gun carry in hotels. No state specifically prohibits carry in hotels. And one state, Montana, actually protects the right of travelers to possess loaded guns in hotel rooms. But, in most states, carry would be subject to the individual policy of the hotel. And this is where the reader should make special note. While a hotel may have a *policy* against gun possession, that policy may lack any "force of law." The hotel can ask a gun-carrying guest to leave. But, unless the guest refuses, no criminal sanctions are possible. The coverage in the Traveler's Checklist is directed toward this common factor. If the hotel is located in a state where a "no gun" policy, with proper "posted" notice, could result in criminal sanctions, then "force of law" is mentioned in the blurb. If a state has a statute allowing rejection or ejectment of a guest for gun possession, this fact is also noted. States with no relevant laws are simply classified as "subject to policy enforcement." Readers should be aware that some states with very strict carry laws (ie. New York & New Jersey) are classified in this way. This does not mean these states are lenient. It simply means that general gun possession is already so stringent that additional laws involving place restrictions are not necessary.

The information in this section assumes that the potential guest is in legal possession of his firearm (preferably with a recognized permit) and is not involved in any other criminal activity. And, while we do not recommend violating even non-criminal hotel policies, necessity may sometimes require that a "judgement call" be made as to whether to keep a gun with you while staying in a hotel. This section will allow one to make an informed decision based on the relevant statutes.

Roadside Rest Areas

Roadside rest areas in almost all states are O.K. for carry unless posted. A few states, such as Illinois, Maryland and New York prohibit carry generally. And Oklahoma prohibits carry in buildings only. But most states recognize gun carry rights at rest areas.

National Parks, Forests and Indian Reservations

Firearm possession in National Parks and wildlife refuges is governed by 16 USC section 1a-7b of the U.S. Code which mandates that gun carry in these areas is regulated by the state where the park or refuge is located. For example, if your permit is recognized in Idaho, you can carry in any park or refuge located in Idaho, subject to the carry restrictions of Idaho. This expansion of the right to carry only applies to outdoor areas such as nature trails and campsites. All official structures such as visitor centers and ranger stations are still off-limits to any gun carry. Private vendors with gift shops and restaurants are not automatically off-limits. But most states allow these entities to post signs that prohibit carry.

National Forests are under the management of the Department of Agriculture and are not subject to the same regulatory action as National Parks. The law of the state where the National Forest is located is usually the law that prevails for gun carry. If a state allows open carry, the National Forests in that state also allow open carry unless otherwise posted. Some travelers have reported "no firearms" signs in National Forests that are located in otherwise firearms-friendly states. These signs may exist because a state's law specifically prohibits carry in a national forest. Or the signs may be posted by officials attempting to enforce an otherwise unenforceable policy. Either way, travelers should know that authorities may enforce these restrictions regardless of their legal basis.

Indian reservations *may have* stricter firearm carry laws within their boundaries than the states where they are located. This condition exists because reservations are relatively autonomous areas that exist as quasi-independent nations. It is beyond the scope of this Guide to cover each reservation specifically. But travelers visiting casinos and other tourist attractions inside reservations would be well-advised to transport all firearms in an unloaded, cased and secure manner that is consistent with the McClure-Volkmer Act discussed earlier. Carry of firearms on one's person is not recommended unless the traveler verifies with the tribal council that such action is lawful.

Motorcycle Issues

Motorcycle riders often ask how carry laws written for four-wheel vehicles apply to them. For example, where is the glove compartment in a motorcycle? Does a saddlebag qualify as a legitimate container for gun carry? Most states' laws do not specifically address these issues. But motorcycle owners can follow some general rules and be sure of compliance in most states.

The rear compartment on a motorcycle qualifies as a trunk if it contains a lock. An unloaded handgun in this locked compartment should be legitimate in most states that prohibit loaded firearms in a vehicle. And, of course, a carry permit would allow the concealed carry of a loaded firearm on one's person in states that recognize the permit. Tote bags have the same effect as a briefcase or gym bag carried on a vehicle's front seat. Most weapons in this venue would be considered concealed.

If one lacks a recognized permit while visiting a state that allows open carry, a firearm could be carried in a hip holster in plain view. This carry mode might appear somewhat aggressive to other motorists and could result in unnecessary attention from police. But it would be an otherwise legal way to carry a handgun in a state that allows open carry. A motorist would have to weigh the advantage of being legally armed with the disadvantage of being subject to increased scrutiny.

Motorhome and RV issues

A common question among RV owners is whether their motorhomes are considered vehicles or residences. Most states consider RVs to be readily mobile and thus subject to all firearm laws concerning vehicular travel. But courts have held that RVs in a fixed state (ie. in a designated campground and hooked up to water, sewer, electric and other utilities) are residences. RV owners should keep this in mind so as to be aware of what their classification is at any one particular time. Many states will allow loaded firearms possession in one's home while prohibiting it in one's vehicle.

Occasional references are made to the trunk transport of firearms. The usual response from RV owners is, "I drive an RV, I don't have a trunk." Because most state statutes do not address the issue of carry in motorhomes, owners should view their external compartments as having the same legal status as a standard vehicle's trunk. A trunk is a compartment that requires one to exit the vehicle in order to gain access to it. If a recommendation is made to transport guns in one's trunk, RVers should take this to mean that transport in a locked, external compartment is legitimate.

The same standard can be applied to trailers. These attachments require one to exit the towing vehicle to access their interiors. Transporting firearms in a trailer would have the same legal effect as transporting firearms in a trunk. Both are separate from the passenger section of the vehicle and would qualify as legitimate storage areas.

Owners of full size RVs sometimes find it difficult to apply the principle of "plain view" carry to their rigs. If the cab is extremely high, how does an approaching police officer see the gun from outside the vehicle? Simply put, the officer cannot. And if the gun is not visible from outside the vehicle, then it is not in plain view. Owners of these motorhomes must exercise another carry option if they wish to keep a loaded gun up front. Many states are allowing console box and glove compartment carry for non-permittees. These options do not have a visibility requirement and probably serve the owners of large motorhomes better than the plain view carry.

And, finally, the practice of "boondocking" or camping in non-designated areas such as Walmart parking lots, has become more common in recent years. Most Rvers resort to this activity without much forethought. You're tired and you need to pullover to get some rest. But what if the property you choose has a "no gun" policy, even in parking areas? It may help to know which states safeguard your gun possession through "parking lot protection" laws. These laws prohibit property owners from extending gun prohibitions to parking areas. If your firearm stays hidden from view within your rig, your right to possess it in your RV is protected in these states. Readers will find this issue covered for each state in the "Traveler's Checklist." The coverage is general and classifies whether a state has comprehensive parking lot protection or not. Some states, like North Carolina, may have protection for permittees in certain specific areas, but no overall protection. For a state to be listed as " *may not prohibit*" the coverage must include most any parking lot open to the public with the exception of K-12 schools which have additional restrictions per federal law – see p.4. Boondockers will find this information helpful. Even though you may still choose to "chance it" in a state that does not have "parking lot protection," you can sleep better knowing your rights.

Traveling by Air, Cruise Ship, Train & Greyhound Bus

While federal law prohibits firearm possession in the sterile areas of airports, persons traveling by air may transport unloaded firearms in their checked baggage. Firearms must be unloaded and secured in locked, hard-sided gun cases. Ammunition should be contained in commercial boxes and not loaded into any extraneous magazines. Firearms and ammunition may be kept in the same locked case unless a specific airline's regulations mandate otherwise. Travelers must notify their airline about the presence of the firearms and/or ammunition when checking the baggage and provide the key to their gun cases if a search is requested. Check-in procedures vary among airlines. Travelers should call ahead to verify where to check-in and what paperwork needs to be completed. Federal law prevents airlines from marking cases containing guns with visible "firearm" signs. Any attempts to do so would be illegal.

Those entering an airport who do not intend to board an airline may carry in the parking lot and non-sterile (before the security screening) terminal areas if allowed by the state where the airport is located. The "Traveler's Checklist" covers this issue on a state by state basis. States that allow carry in both terminals and parking lots are noted as well as states that allow carry in parking lots only. Some states prohibit carry on all airport property and others may allow localities to decide the matter. Those exercising this option must be lawfully allowed to carry (ie. by permit or other authorization) in the state where the airport is located. They must also watch for postings that indicate where "sterile areas" begin and where "no weapon" zones are located.

A federal court recently held that the interstate transportation protections of McClure-Volkmer (p.5) only apply to vehicular travel. Travelers with connecting flights through restrictive states could face local prosecution if they possess any firearms that are illegal in those states.

Gun owners traveling by train, cruise ship, greyhound bus or other form of common carrier involved in interstate transportation must turn over possession of their legally owned firearms and ammunition to the captain, conductor or pilot of the vessel for the duration of the trip. Certain carriers will make provisions for passengers transporting firearms. But travelers are encouraged to contact the carrier before making passage to determine what that policy might be.

Over the Road Commercial Trucks

Mark Twain once said, "a rumor is half way around the world before the truth gets its boots on." One of the most often heard rumors is that federal law prohibits carrying firearms in commercial vehicles such as semi-tractor trailers. This myth has been repeated by trucking company supervisors and corporate management for years with no legal citation or statutory proof offered for support. The truth is that while many companies have internal policies that prohibit guns in company vehicles, no federal law exists that regulates guns in trucks. Truckers can carry subject to the same state and local restrictions as everyone else. Independent truckers will have an easier time carrying simply because they are not beholden to company polices that may prohibit such activity. But any trucker, regardless of company policy, ***will not*** be violating federal law if he carries a gun for personal protection.

Current & Retired Law Enforcement Officers

Federal law allows all active duty law enforcement officers from any state or locality to carry concealed firearms while traveling. The officer must possess an official photographic identification from his department and be authorized to carry a firearm by the agency with which he is employed. The firearm may be carried in most public areas but must remain concealed. This carry allowance does not extend to any governmental property where carry is prohibited or private properties where the owners restrict gun possession. State magazine restrictions apply to officers who carry under this law. But recent amendments exempt officers from any ammunition restrictions that are not rooted in federal law.

Retired law enforcement officers also have the right to carry concealed firearms while traveling in the same manner stated above. But the restrictions on their qualifying status are much greater. To be considered a "retired law enforcement officer," one must have been employed as a law enforcement officer for at least 10 years and been authorized during that period to carry a firearm and conduct arrests and investigations. If an officer did not achieve a full 10 years of service, but separated from employment early because of a service connected disability, then any probationary service period as determined by his department of employment would be acceptable. Most importantly, every 12 months, a retired officer must meet his current state's firearm qualification standards for police or those standards of the agency from which he retired. He must also have a photographic identification issued by the department from which he retired identifying him as a former policeman of that department. Certification through either the agency he retired from or any certified firearms instructor or law enforcement agency in his current state of residence is acceptable.

Preemption of Local Laws

Firearm preemption laws prevent cities and counties from regulating the carry, possession and ownership of firearms. Some laws mandate total uniformity by prohibiting any amount of home rule while others *grandfather* preexisting local ordinances. A small minority allows limited local control in certain areas (ie. open carry). These distinctions are noted for each state and help the traveler determine if issues such as open carry or glove compartment placement are subject to local control. Travelers will find their journeys much easier to plan in states with comprehensive preemption laws in place.

We hope readers will benefit from the information discussed in the proceeding pages. Travel with firearms in the United States is as much a necessity as a guaranteed right. Knowing how to carry your firearms in a legally correct manner is as essential to safe, efficient travel as a good road atlas.

Use a colored pencil to shade the states where your permit is recognized

Alabama

Total prohibition *(+0, good state for permittees, but travel is tougher for those without)* **Total freedom**

0 ------- 10 ------- 20 ------- 30 ------- 40 ------- 50 ------- 60 ------- 70 ------- 80 ------ 90 ------ 100

^

CHECKLIST

***Standard firearms & ammo:** no permit required for possession or sale – see p. 3
***Semi-auto guns & high capacity magazines:** no permit required for possession or sale
***Machine guns & suppressors:** ownership lawful per federal law compliance
***Firearm law uniformity:** uniform throughout state, local unit liability for non-compliance
***Right of Self-Defense:** NRA-model castle doctrine, *stand your ground* in public areas
***Open carry:** unrestricted in most public areas; some exceptions, see below
***Licensed concealed carry:** licenses issued by sheriffs on a "shall issue" basis to residents only
***Constitutional or "no permit required" concealed carry:** no
***Out-of-state permit recognition:** automatic recognition for all nonresidents with carry permits
***Weapons allowed for *licensed* carry:** limited to handguns only

VEHICLES

***Vehicle carry by non-permittees:** handguns must be unloaded and cased in the trunk or storage area; loaded long guns may be in plain view or gun cases (some exceptions, see below)
***Vehicle gun possession at colleges:** subject to college administrative policy
***Vehicle gun possession at K-12 schools:** subject to policy enforcement by local school boards
***Duty to notify LEO of permit status:** upon demand of police officer
***RV carry while "boondocking":** parking lot owners may restrict gun carry by visitors – see p.8

***State Parks:** concealed handgun carry by recognized licensees permitted
***Restaurants serving alcohol:** permittees may carry while eating in dining areas – see p.3
***Hotels:** subject to hotel policy enforcement – see p.7
***Airports:** carry allowed in non-sterile terminal areas and parking lots – see p. 9

The "Heart of Dixie" has a well-earned reputation for a strong and vibrant gun culture. Visitors will find Alabama's laws stricter than some other states of the Cotton Belt but generally conducive to unmolested travel.

Recognized permittees: A license is required to carry a handgun in a vehicle or concealed on or about one's person. A resident's local sheriff issues such licenses on a "shall issue" basis for one to five year terms. Alabama does not issue permits to nonresidents but will recognize any out-of-state carry permit so long as the permittee is a nonresident.

A recognized licensee may carry a loaded, concealed handgun in most public areas. Alabama even has legal exceptions for permittee carry in K-12 school facilities, subject to policy enforcement by local school boards. But, despite this relative freedom, postings prohibiting carry may exist for certain public buildings, some universally restricted areas (p.7) and restricted access facilities (see All Persons).

Persons without recognized permits: A non-permittee may not carry a loaded, readily accessible handgun in a vehicle or concealed on or about his person. This would include placing a handgun under one's coat as well as hiding the weapon in a purse, briefcase or gym bag. While traveling in a vehicle, all handguns should be unloaded, cased and secured in the trunk or rear storage area. Glove compartment, console box and "under the seat" carry are not allowed.

All Persons: Loaded long guns in plain view or secured in cases may be transported in vehicles throughout most of the state. But certain areas, such as state parks, state land division properties and wildlife management areas, require all long guns in vehicles to be unloaded. .

Anyone may openly carry a loaded handgun while on foot in most public areas. Open carry on private property requires a carry license or the consent of the property's owner. And travelers may find some public and private parking lots off-limits to gun possession, even if the gun is kept within one's vehicle.

Buildings with restricted access (turnstiles, metal detectors, etc.), law enforcement offices, hospitals and courthouses are also prohibited. But these places must post signs and may not prohibit visitors from having guns secured in closed compartments in their cars. Athletic events are O.K. for permittees unless the facilities are "restricted access" areas. Then the prohibition applies to everyone. And firearms carry at or near public demonstrations is prohibited.

Alaska

Total prohibition *(+0, America's frontier, great for guns, need we say more)* **Total freedom**

0 ------- 10 ------- 20 ------- 30 ------- 40 ------- 50 ------- 60 ------- 70 ------- 80 ------ 90 ------ 100

^

CHECKLIST

***Standard firearms & ammo:** no permit required for possession or sale – see p. 3
***Semi-auto guns & high capacity magazines:** no permit required for possession or sale
***Machine guns & suppressors:** ownership lawful per federal law compliance
***Firearm law uniformity:** preemption statute, localities prohibited from regulating any aspect of firearms possession and carry
***Right of Self-Defense:** NRA model castle doctrine, *stand your ground* in public areas
***Open carry:** unrestricted under state law, generally accepted in most areas
***Licensed concealed carry:** licenses granted to residents on a "shall issue" basis
***Constitutional or "no permit required" concealed carry:** yes – see below
***Out-of-state permit recognition:** automatic recognition of carry permits from all other states
***Weapons allowed for *licensed* carry:** limited to handguns only

VEHICLES

***Vehicle carry by non-permittees:** loaded, concealed firearms may be carried anywhere in a vehicle by persons 21 years or older
***Vehicle gun possession at colleges:** lawful for any gun owner
***Vehicle gun possession at K-12 schools:** Alaska permittee must unload and encase gun
***Duty to notify LEO of permit/carry status:** immediately upon official contact
***RV carry while "boondocking":** parking lot owners may *not* prohibit guns in vehicles – see p.8

***State Parks:** any non-felon may carry a firearm for self-defense
***Restaurant serving alcohol:** concealed handgun carry O.K. in dining areas – see p.3
***Hotels:** subject to hotel policy enforcement & possible "force of law" posting prohibitions – see p. 7
***Airports:** carry allowed in non-sterile terminal areas and parking lots – see p. 9

The Alaskan frontier remains a permanent part of life for most of the population. This condition makes gun ownership a popular pursuit for the state's nearly 700,000 residents. Travelers to our northern boundary will experience few problems cruising the state's tundra.

Recognized permittees: Alaska grants carry permits to residents on a "shall issue" basis and recognizes permits issued by any other state or locality. A permit is issued for a five-year term and authorizes the holder to carry a loaded, concealed handgun in most public areas. The need for a permit was diminished in 2003 when the state adopted a Vermont-style carry policy that allows any person 21 years or older to carry a concealed handgun without a license. Licenses are still issued so Alaskans can enjoy reciprocal privileges while traveling.

Persons without recognized permits: Any person who is 21 years or older may carry a concealed, loaded handgun in the passenger compartment of his vehicle or in most public areas while on foot. This allowance extends to a handgun concealed under one's coat or in a gym bag, purse or briefcase carried by the person. While in a vehicle, console box, glove compartment and "under the seat" placement are also legitimate.

All Persons: Firearms carry is prohibited in bars, K-12 schools, day care & assisted living centers. Gun carry in private residences is also prohibited unless the owner of the property provides express permission for such carry. But a traveler who is not otherwise prohibited from possessing firearms may carry a concealed handgun in a restaurant as long as he does not consume any liquor. Any person carrying a concealed firearm must always inform a police officer who contacts that person for an official purpose that he is armed.

Loaded rifles and shotguns may be carried by anyone while on foot or being transported in a vehicle. Gun racks and gun cases are the most common methods of stowage in vehicles.

Local regulation of firearm issues is prohibited. A comprehensive preemption statute prohibits localities from regulating any aspect of firearm carry, transportation, ownership, or possession. Private businesses and most state and municipal properties are also prohibited from regulating firearm possession in vehicles parked on their premises. This aspect, coupled with the unrestrictive carry laws noted above, makes Alaska one of America's most gun-friendly states.

Arizona

Total prohibition *(+0, wide open desert & constitutional carry make it one of our best)* **Total freedom**

0 ------- 10 ------- 20 ------- 30 ------- 40 ------- 50 ------- 60 ------- 70 ------- 80 ------ 90 ------ 100

^ (100)

CHECKLIST

***Standard firearms & ammo:** no permit required for possession or sale – see p. 3
***Semi-auto guns & high capacity magazines:** no permit required for possession or sale
***Machine guns & suppressors:** ownership lawful per federal law compliance
***Firearm law uniformity:** localities prohibited from enacting or enforcing laws regulating most forms of gun carry; cities may suffer civil penalties for violating preemption (see below)
***Right of Self-Defense:** NRA-model castle doctrine, *stand your ground* in public areas
***Open carry:** unrestricted under state law in most public areas and generally accepted
***Licensed concealed carry:** licenses issued to qualified U.S. citizens on a "shall issue" basis
***Constitutional or "no permit required" concealed carry:** yes – see below
***Out-of-state permit recognition:** automatic recognition of carry permits from all other states
***Weapons allowed for *licensed* carry:** include any lawful deadly weapon

VEHICLES

***Vehicle carry by non-permittees:** loaded firearms may be carried either concealed or openly by anyone who is law-abiding and 21 years or older
***Vehicle gun possession at colleges:** lawful for any gun owner (permittee or non-permittee)
***Vehicle gun possession at K-12 schools:** Arizona permittee w/**unloaded** handgun lawful
***Duty to notify LEO of permit/carry status:** upon demand of police officer
***RV carry while "boondocking":** parking lot owners may *not* prohibit guns in vehicles – see p.8

***State Parks:** concealed handgun carry by recognized licensees permitted
***Restaurants serving alcohol:** permittees may carry while eating in dining areas – see p.3
***Hotels:** subject to hotel policy enforcement & "force of law" posting prohibitions -- see p.7
***Airports:** carry allowed in non-sterile terminal areas and parking lots – see p.9

It is not uncommon to see citizens walking the streets of major Arizona cities with holstered, loaded firearms. While open carry without a permit may be legal in other states as well, it is perhaps more commonly practiced in the Grand Canyon State than elsewhere. And, thanks to pro-gun legislators, Arizona extends this freedom to concealed carry. Arizona is one of a growing number of states where a citizen need not obtain a government permission slip (aka permit) to carry a concealed weapon.

Recognized permittees: Despite having "permitless" concealed carry, Arizona still issues licenses to carry concealed weapons on a "shall issue" basis to Arizona residents or qualified U.S. citizens for five-year terms. Arizona recognizes any other state's permit so long as the permittee is legally present in the state, has physical possession of his license and is at least 21 years of age with no outstanding indictments or warrants.

Certain advantages exist to having a permit. For example, carry is allowed in restaurants that serve alcohol unless the owner of the business posts a sign prohibiting carry. Persons without permits may not carry concealed or openly regardless of posting. And most residents find that out-of-state travel is much easier with a carry license. Many states that still require a license to carry will recognize the Arizona permit.

Persons without recognized permits: Anyone who is law-abiding and at least 21 years old may carry a concealed weapon in his vehicle or on foot in most public areas. He must disclose to police, if asked, that he has a firearm. And he may not carry into any business serving alcohol for consumption on the premises.

All Persons: Arizona's preemption statute prevents localities from enacting or enforcing most laws regulating firearms and provides civil penalties for violators. Persons are still prohibited from carry in such obvious areas as K-12 schools, polling booths on Election Day and nuclear & hydroelectric power plants. Carry *may* be banned in some less obvious areas such as "public establishments" (ie. sports arena owned or leased by the government) and "public events" (ie. outdoor music concerts). Public establishments must post signs that notify visitors of any carry prohibitions and must also provide secure storage for firearms during the duration of one's visit. Public events must be licensed events and do not include informal gatherings of people. Fortunately for travelers, most property owners are prohibited from enforcing rules that ban firearms in privately owned vehicles in their parking lots. And schools and universities are prohibited from enforcing policies that prohibit lawful gun possession in vehicles located in public right-of-ways around their properties.

Arkansas

Total prohibition ***(+0, guns, football & pickups are essential in Razorback country)*** **Total freedom**

0 ------- 10 ------- 20 ------- 30 ------- 40 ------- 50 ------- 60 ------- 70 ------- 80 ------ 90 ------ 100

^

CHECKLIST

***Standard firearms & ammo:** no permit required for possession or sale – see p. 3
***Semi-auto guns & high capacity magazines:** no permit required for possession or sale
***Machine guns & suppressors:** ownership lawful per federal law compliance
***Firearm law uniformity:** preemption statute; laws mostly uniform throughout state
***Right of Self-Defense:** NRA-model castle doctrine, but *duty to retreat* in public areas
***Open carry:** lawful in public areas where firearms are not specifically prohibited – see below
***Licensed concealed carry:** licenses issued on a "shall issue" basis to residents only
***Constitutional or "no permit required" concealed carry:** yes – see below
***Out-of-state permit recognition:** automatic recognition of carry permits from all other states
***Weapons allowed for *licensed* carry:** limited to handguns only

VEHICLES

***Vehicle carry by non-permittees:** recent court decision supports loaded handguns anywhere in vehicle (see below); long guns may be in plain view or secured in commercial gun cases
***Vehicle gun possession at colleges:** prohibited if posted, otherwise lawful for permittees
***Vehicle gun possession at K-12 schools:** Arkansas permittee w/loaded handgun lawful so long as parking lot is *publicly* owned (private schools set their own rules)
***Duty to notify LEO of permit/carry status:** immediately upon contact and request for ID
***RV carry while "boondocking":** parking lot owners may restrict gun carry by visitors – see p.8
***State Parks:** recognized licensees may carry in open areas, but not in any gov't buildings
***Restaurants serving alcohol:** permittees may carry while eating in dining areas – p.3
***Hotels:** subject to hotel policy enforcement & "force of law" posting prohibitions – see p.7
***Airports:** carry prohibited in passenger terminals; car carry in parking lots O.K. – see p.9

Arkansas's reputation as a rough and ready frontier state in the late 1850s fostered a climate where many a Civil War battle was fought between citizens with opposing sympathies. Privately owned firearms played a key role in determining the outcome of these skirmishes.

Recognized permittees: The State Police issues permits to carry concealed handguns to qualified residents who are least 21 years old. Permits are granted for five-year terms and only allow the carry of *concealed* handguns. Permittees may upgrade their licenses to "enhanced" status by completing additional training. Enhanced permittees may then carry in many of the otherwise prohibited areas listed below. Arkansas will not grant permits to nonresidents but will recognize carry permits from all other states. Permittees must inform a police officer upon contact that they are carrying a handgun.

A permittee may carry a concealed handgun in a vehicle or on his person in most public areas. But churches (absent consent of church leaders), K-12 public schools (private K-12 set their own rules), college buildings & courthouses (except for some staff), athletic events, parades, bars, state offices (including those in state parks), publicly-owned buildings (except rest area), governmental meetings, airports and police stations are off-limits to carry. Most other "prohibited" areas are posted. Publicly-owned parking lots for these areas are O.K. if the handgun remains locked in the permittees' vehicle. Arkansas "enhanced" permittees may carry in many of the above areas (including college bldgs.). But enhancement is limited to Arkansas residents. And the specifics of such carry are too detailed for coverage here.

Persons without recognized permits: Arkansas prohibits carrying a handgun on or about one's person or in a vehicle if the purpose is to *unlawfully* employ it as a "weapon." The Arkansas Court of Appeals (October, 2018) confirmed that this language allows the possession of a loaded handgun in a vehicle and the carry of one while on foot as long as the carrier does not intend to use the handgun to commit a criminal offense. Those who carry without a permit should observe all carry restrictions listed above for permittees and be aware that most exceptions to these restrictions (ie. vehicle possession on prohibited property) still require a permit.

All Persons: Shotguns and rifles may be carried in gun racks or commercial gun cases but should remain unloaded during hunting season. Permittees are only authorized to carry handguns with their licenses. And the newly confirmed permitless carry only applies to handguns.

California

Total prohibition *(+0, this once Reagan-friendly state is now a gulag for gun owners)* **Total freedom**

0 ------- 10 ------- 20 ------- 30 ------- 40 ------- 50 ------- 60 ------- 70 ------- 80 ------ 90 ------ 100

^

CHECKLIST

- ***Standard firearms & ammo:** firearm registration required for all *new* residents; ammo sales regulated, but possession *generally* unrestricted under state law – see p. 3
- ***Semi-auto guns & high capacity magazines:** restricted, all guns deemed "assault weapons" prohibited; magazines over 10 shots may not be imported; bump stocks prohibited
- ***Machine guns & suppressors:** personal ownership prohibited
- ***Firearm law uniformity:** limited preemption law, some areas of local regulation may exist
- ***Right of Self-Defense:** no NRA-model castle doctrine; self-defense rules based on jury instructions
- ***Open carry:** prohibited in all public areas (loaded or unloaded)
- ***Licensed concealed carry:** licenses issued on a "may issue" basis by sheriffs to residents only
- ***Constitutional or "no permit required" concealed carry:** no
- ***Out-of-state permit recognition:** no recognition of out-of-state carry permits
- ***Weapons allowed for *licensed* carry:** limited to handguns only

VEHICLES

- ***Vehicle carry by non-permittees:** handguns must be unloaded and secured in a *locked* trunk or *locked* utility box or *locked* in gun cases; long guns must be unloaded
- ***Vehicle gun possession at colleges:** firearm possession prohibited by law
- ***Vehicle gun possession at K-12 schools:** firearms must be unloaded & in locked cases
- ***Duty to notify LEO of permit status:** upon demand of police officer
- ***RV carry while "boondocking":** parking lot owners may restrict gun carry by visitors – see p.8

- ***State Parks:** firearms must be cased, unloaded and kept within a vehicle or campsite
- ***Restaurants serving alcohol:** permittees may carry while eating in dining areas – see p.3
- ***Hotels:** statutory exception for loaded guns, but policy enforcement still possible – see p.7
- ***Airports:** carry in non-sterile terminal areas and parking lots O.K., but watch for local postings: see p.9

Changing demographics and a left wing political agenda in Sacramento has made the once Reagan-friendly State of California a nightmare for travelers carrying firearms.

California permittees: The state requires a California-issued license to carry a handgun concealed on your person or loaded and concealed in a vehicle. California does not issue permits to nonresidents and will not recognize out-of-state licenses. But sheriffs will issue permits to residents for "good cause" and may impose additional carry restrictions on the licenses they issue. Permittees are prohibited from carry at gun shows, the state capitol, polling booths, public demonstrations, courtrooms, K-12 schools, colleges and any posted areas.

Persons without California permits: Vehicle transport of a handgun is limited to an unloaded handgun *locked* in the trunk or permanently-affixed utility box. An unloaded handgun may also be transported in the passenger compartment if it is secured in a *locked* gun case. Handguns may not be kept in the glove compartment or console box. Rifles and shotguns must be unloaded but need not be in locked containers. Transportation in gun cases is recommended. "Loaded" is when ammunition is in a firearm's chamber or any attached magazine. Ammunition should be kept in separate containers.

Open carry of loaded firearms on foot is prohibited in most public areas. Specific exceptions exist which allow licensed hunters to carry loaded firearms while engaged in hunting and shooters to carry while at designated target ranges. Carry at campsites or temporary residences such as hotel rooms or "in camp" RVs is also lawful as long as possession does not conflict with an intervening local or federal law. RVs on public roads would not qualify for this exception. But RVs hooked into utilities at a campground would be legitimate.

Open carry of any *unloaded* firearm is also prohibited in most public areas of both incorporated and unincorporated areas. And while such carry is lawful for licensed hunters while hunting and target shooters while shooting at designated ranges, any defensive carry in public areas is prohibited.

All Persons: California prevents localities from regulating most aspects of gun licensing and registration. But state prohibitions on the importation of semi-automatic assault weapons, .50 caliber center-fire rifles and over 10 shot magazines continue to show the cumulative effect of decades of state-sanctioned gun control.

Colorado

Total prohibition *(+0, despite Denver, Colorado is still pro-gun)* **Total freedom**

0 ------- 10 ------- 20 ------- 30 ------- 40 ------- 50 ------- 60 ------- 70 ------- 80 ------ 90 ------ 100

^

C H E C K L I S T

***Standard firearms & ammo:** no permit required for possession or sale – see p. 3
***Semi-auto guns & high capacity magazines:** over 15 shot magazines not lawfully possessed on July 1, 2013 prohibited; semi-auto guns restricted in some localities such as Denver
***Machine guns & suppressors:** ownership lawful per federal law compliance
***Firearm law uniformity:** preemption law, localities prohibited from enforcing *most* ordinances regulating guns, but some notable exceptions exist - see below
***Right of Self-Defense:** NRA castle doctrine, but *stand your ground* in public not codified
***Open carry:** unrestricted under state law; localities may regulate this aspect independently
***Licensed concealed carry:** licenses issued by sheriffs on a "shall issue" basis to residents only
***Constitutional or "no permit required" concealed carry:** no
***Out-of-state permit recognition:** conditional recognition of permits from other states (see p. 65)
***Weapons allowed for *licensed* carry:** limited to handguns only

V E H I C L E S

***Vehicle carry by non-permittees:** firearms may be lawfully carried anywhere in a vehicle; handguns may be loaded, rifles and shotguns must be unloaded – see below
***Vehicle gun possession at colleges:** lawful for permittees and their handguns only
***Vehicle gun possession at K-12 schools:** Colorado permittee w/loaded handgun lawful
***Duty to notify LEO of permit status:** upon demand of police officer
***RV carry while "boondocking":** parking lot owners may restrict gun carry by visitors – see p.8

***State Parks:** concealed carry of handguns by recognized licensees permitted
***Restaurants serving alcohol:** permittees may carry while eating in dining areas – see p.3
***Hotels:** subject to hotel policy enforcement – see p. 7
***Airports:** carry allowed in non-sterile terminal areas and parking lots – see p.9

Colorado still maintains a strong western tradition with guns. Despite an influx of liberal "refugees' from California, the state's gun laws continue to reflect the best of the Rocky Mountain West.

Recognized permittees: A license is required to carry a concealed handgun while on foot. The sheriff of a person's home county issues such a permit for a five-year term. Colorado does not issue licenses to nonresidents but will recognize permits issued by states that recognize Colorado permits. Out-of-state permittees must be at least 21 years old and residents of the state that issued the permit (as evidenced by a driver's license) for their carry permits to be valid. Permittees are authorized to carry concealed in most public areas except K-12 schools and public buildings with security screenings.

Persons without recognized permits: A loaded handgun may be carried for self-defense anywhere in a vehicle. Open carry is legitimate everywhere but Denver. The city mandates that all firearms in a vehicle remain concealed from view and any hunting weapons remain unloaded.

While on foot, a non-permittee engaged in lawful hunting activities may carry a concealed handgun. Colorado allows open carry in most public areas with three notable exceptions. Localities may prohibit the open carry of handguns in buildings and specific outdoor areas by posting conspicuous signs. Denver limits any personal carry on foot to those who carry concealed with recognized permits. And firearms carry on public transportation is prohibited unless one possesses a recognized license.

All Persons: Long guns may be transported in a vehicle if they are unloaded. "Unloaded" applies only to a weapon's chamber. The magazines may contain live rounds. But those transporting firearms in a snowmobile must also unload their magazines and secure the guns in cases.

Colorado's magazine ban only affects over 15 shot magazines that were not lawfully owned prior to July 1, 2013. Magazines purchased or possessed before this date are lawful. And with most Colorado sheriffs opposing this ban, strict enforcement is spotty at best.

Some cities, such as Denver and Boulder, restrict possession of semi-auto weapons by their residents. But nonresidents transporting such weapons in private vehicles are exempt from enforcement. And Aurora recently began enforcing criminal penalties against anyone that carries onto posted property.

Connecticut

Total prohibition ***(+0, the bad gets worse as gunmakers leave the state in droves)*** **Total freedom**

0 ------- 10 ------- 20 ------- 30 ------- 40 ------- 50 ------- 60 ------- 70 ------- 80 ------ 90 ------ 100

^ (at 10)

CHECKLIST

***Standard firearms & ammo:** permit or certificate required for all transfers of guns and ammo

***Semi-auto guns & high capacity magazines:** importation of any over 10 shot magazine or any "assault weapon" (anything that looks remotely military) is prohibited

***Machine guns & suppressors:** heavily restricted, importation of machine guns prohibited; "bump stocks" prohibited; suppressor ownership lawful per federal law compliance

***Firearm law uniformity:** no preemption statute; local laws may exist in some areas

***Right of Self-Defense:** no NRA-model castle doctrine, *duty to retreat* in public areas

***Open carry:** prohibited in all public areas unless one has a Connecticut permit

***Licensed concealed carry:** licenses issued on a "may issue" basis to residents and nonresidents

***Constitutional or "no permit required" concealed carry:** no

***Out-of-state permit recognition:** no general recognition of out-of-state carry permits

***Weapons allowed for *licensed* carry:** limited to handguns only

VEHICLES

***Vehicle carry by non-permittees:** handgun carry prohibited absent exception; loaded rifles and shotguns prohibited (see below)

***Vehicle gun possession at colleges:** subject to college administrative policy

***Vehicle gun possession at K-12 schools:** firearm possession prohibited

***Duty to notify LEO of permit status:** upon demand of police officer

***RV carry while "boondocking":** parking lot owners may restrict gun carry by visitors – see p.8

***State Parks:** firearms carry prohibited

***Restaurants serving alcohol:** permittees may carry while eating in dining areas – see p.3

***Hotels:** subject to policy enforcement & "force of law" posting prohibitions (possible felony) – see p. 7

***Airports:** carry in non-sterile terminal areas & parking lots O.K., but watch for local postings – see p.9

Connecticut's gun laws have become more severe over the last twenty years. While residents and nonresidents alike may acquire handgun carry permits through the state police, anyone who lacks a Connecticut permit faces an unfriendly environment for gun carry.

Connecticut permittees: Vehicle carry of any handgun requires a Connecticut carry permit. The state police issue these permits after a resident has first obtained a temporary permit from his hometown. A nonresident with a carry permit from his home state may travel to an officially recognized gun competition or collectors exhibition if he transports his unloaded handgun in a *locked* case or in the vehicle's trunk or inaccessible storage area. He should also have proof of the event (ie. registration form).

Any U. S. citizen who possesses a carry license issued by another state may apply directly to the state police for a Connecticut permit. Such licenses are valid for five years, cost $70.00 + processing fees and allow concealed and open carry. A recent law change now requires permittees to keep their handguns in "locked" compartments when their vehicles are unoccupied.

And, aside from prohibiting carry in K-12 schools and the State Capitol, Connecticut allows localities to enforce their own laws on firearms. Many cities are enacting ordinances that restrict carry. Watch for postings.

Persons without Connecticut permits: Vehicle carry of a handgun is prohibited without a Connecticut permit. Exceptions exist which allow the transport of unloaded handguns in locked containers from place of purchase to home, etc. But general car carry is prohibited.

Long guns in a vehicle must be unloaded and, in the case of a resident with a grandfathered assault weapon, locked in a case or trunk with a certificate of registration. The courts have interpreted Connecticut law very strictly with regards to the vehicle transport of firearms. Non-resident travelers should only possess firearms that are securely cased and unloaded per McClure-Volkmer (p. 5) or state statute *29-38d* that mirrors the federal law.

All Persons: Lack of state preemption means that most localities have ordinances prohibiting carry in public parks and government buildings. All ammunition and gun transfers require a permit or certificate issued by Connecticut. And importation into the state of any "semi-automatic assault weapon," over 10 shot magazine or "bump stock" is prohibited.

Delaware

Total prohibition ***(+0, better than some of its neighbors, but room for improvement)*** **Total freedom**

0 ------- 10 ------- 20 ------- 30 ------- 40 ------- 50 ------- 60 ------- 70 ------- 80 ------ 90 ------ 100

^

CHECKLIST

***Standard firearms & ammo:** no permit required for possession or sale – see p.3
***Semi-auto guns & high capacity magazines:** no permit required for possession or sale
***Machine guns & suppressors:** personal ownership prohibited
***Firearm law uniformity:** state preemption law, pre-85 laws grandfathered; localities have power to enact new laws regulating open carry in local gov't bldgs.; bump stocks prohibited
***Right of Self-Defense:** no NRA-model castle doctrine, *duty to retreat* in public areas
***Open carry:** unrestricted; however, local ordinances prohibiting open carry may exist
***Licensed concealed carry:** licenses issued on a "may issue" basis to residents only
***Constitutional or "no permit required" concealed carry:** no
***Out-of-state permit recognition:** conditional recognition of permits from other states (see p. 65)
***Weapons allowed for *licensed* concealed carry:** include any lawful deadly weapon

VEHICLES

***Vehicle carry by non-permittees:** a loaded handgun may be carried openly or secured in the trunk; rifles and shotguns must be unloaded while in a vehicle
***Vehicle gun possession at colleges:** subject to college administrative policy
***Vehicle gun possession at K-12 schools:** Delaware permittee w/loaded handgun lawful
***Duty to notify LEO of permit status:** upon demand of police officer
***RV carry while "boondocking":** parking lot owners may restrict gun carry by visitors – see p.8

***State Parks:** Delaware permittee may carry anywhere in park; other permittees limited – see below
***Restaurants serving alcohol:** permittees may carry while eating in dining areas – see p.3
***Hotels:** subject to hotel policy enforcement – see p.7
***Airports:** carry in non-sterile terminal areas & parking lots O.K., but watch for local postings – see p.9

Delaware's proximity to northeast liberalism might lead one to suppose that the state's gun laws are as strict as those of New York. Delaware's rural character, however, has helped preserve a laissez-faire view toward firearm ownership uncommon on the Northeast Coast.

Recognized permittees: The state requires a license to carry a concealed firearm. Such permits are issued to residents through the local superior court of each county and allow the concealed, loaded carry of a handgun within a vehicle or on foot in most public areas. Licenses are initially granted for a period of three years and can then be renewed for five years. Delaware does not issue permits to nonresidents but recognizes licenses of nonresidents from states that provide reasonably similar standards for issuance and also recognize Delaware's permits. Permittees may carry firearms in most public areas of the state (see "all persons" below).

Persons without recognized permits: A loaded handgun may be in a vehicle if the weapon is in plain view (ie. seat or dashboard) or stored in an inaccessible area such as the trunk. Handguns *may not* be carried in the glove compartment or console box or concealed anywhere on or about one's person.

While on foot, a handgun may be carried openly in a visible belt holster. Because carrying a concealed weapon without a license is a felony, non-licensed travelers who carry openly should exercise caution while carrying. State preemption is broad enough to prohibit most local gun regulation. But ordinances predating 1985 are grandfathered. And localities are empowered to enact new carry restrictions for their govt. buildings.

All Persons: Shotguns and rifles must be unloaded when transported in any motorized vehicle or watercraft and properly secured in a rear window gun rack or commercial gun case. Long guns must be unloaded regardless of whether a person has a permit. Although Delaware's licensing law technically allows the carry of any firearm by those with recognized permits, long guns are further regulated by conservation laws and must remain unloaded while in a vehicle.

Anyone is prohibited from possessing firearms in courthouses, law enforcement offices and federal buildings (per p.7). Delaware permittees may carry in most areas of state parks and forests. But out-of-state permittees (absent permission of Director) and those without permits are generally barred from carry in "designated areas" which include visitor centers, campgrounds, playgrounds etc.

District of Columbia

Total prohibition ***(+0, despite reluctant leaders, court-mandated "shall issue" continues)*** **Total freedom**

0 ------- 10 ------- 20 ------- 30 ------- 40 ------- 50 ------- 60 ------- 70 ------- 80 ------ 90 ------ 100

^

CHECKLIST

***Standard firearms & ammo:** restricted, guns & ammo prohibited absent D.C. issued certificate
***Semi-auto guns & high capacity magazines:** prohibited; ownership of any military-pattern weapon or over 10-shot magazine unlawful
***Machine guns & suppressors:** prohibited; ownership of any Class III item unlawful
***Firearm law uniformity:** laws are uniformly strict throughout the district
***Right of Self-Defense:** no NRA-model castle doctrine; duty to retreat based on case law (although not explicit, duty to retreat practically exists for most public places)
***Open carry:** prohibited anywhere in the District
***Licensed concealed carry:** licenses issued to residents and non-residents through the chief of police; recent court decision has forced D.C. to adopt "shall issue" licensing
***Constitutional or "no permit required" concealed carry:** no
***Out-of-state permit recognition:** no recognition of out-of-state carry permits
***Weapons allowed for *licensed* carry:** limited to handguns only

VEHICLES

***Vehicle carry by non-permittees:** firearms must be unloaded, cased and locked in the trunk; vehicles without trunks may use locked containers (see below)
***Vehicle gun possession at colleges:** prohibited by law
***Vehicle gun possession at K-12 schools:** firearm possession prohibited
***Duty to notify LEO of permit status:** immediately upon official contact
***RV carry while "boondocking":** parking lot owners may restrict gun carry by visitors – see p.8

***State Parks:** n/a
***Restaurants serving alcohol:** permittees may carry in dining area unless posted
***Hotels:** subject to hotel policy enforcement & "force of law" posting prohibitions– see p.7
***Airports:** n/a (no airport in D.C. – see Virginia)

In 2014, D.C. city council enacted emergency legislation providing for the issuance of concealed carry licenses to qualified persons. The resulting law was highly restrictive and practically ineffective. A recent U.S. Court of Appeals decision, however, found that this "may issue" licensing system violated the Second Amendment. D.C. has since been forced to adopt "shall issue" licensing.

Washington D.C. permittees: A license is required to carry a concealed pistol on one's person or in a vehicle. Such permits are issued by the Chief of Police to qualified persons who are at least 21 years old for 2 year terms. Until recently, applicants had to demonstrate a specific personal need for a license. This requirement has been struck down. And now D.C. is in the process of granting permits on a "shall issue" basis.

The District will not recognize carry permits issued by other states but will issue permits to residents and non-residents. Licensees may only carry *concealed* handguns that are secured in holsters with no more than 20 rounds of ammunition on their persons at one time. Licensees are prohibited from carry in most public areas including government buildings, schools & colleges, churches, child care facilities, hospitals, public transportation (including Metrorail), public gatherings & demonstrations, bars, stadiums, public memorials, and all private residences (absent owner consent). Any licensee approaching these prohibited areas must immediately unload his handgun and secure it in his locked vehicle. Permittees must also declare their permit status upon any official contact with law enforcement.

Non-Residents without D.C. permits: Those without D.C. permits are prohibited from carrying any firearms or ammunition in the District. Such items may be transported *through* the District if the firearms are unloaded, cased and locked in the trunk or, in a vehicle without a trunk, secured in a locked container (other than a glove compartment or console box). Any ammunition must be separate from the guns. And the traveler may not stop anywhere in the District.

Recent reports indicate that persons have been arrested for having one spent ammunition cartridge in the passenger compartment of their vehicle. Anyone traveling *through* the District should exercise extreme caution when transporting firearms or ammunition.

Florida

Total prohibition *(+0, remains pro-gun despite shifting demographics)* **Total freedom**

0 ------- 10 ------- 20 ------- 30 ------- 40 ------- 50 ------- 60 ------- 70 ------- 80 ------ 90 ------ 100

^ (90)

CHECKLIST

- ***Standard firearms & ammo:** no permit required for possession or sale – see p.3
- ***Semi-auto guns & high capacity magazines:** no permit required for possession or sale
- ***Machine guns & suppressors:** ownership lawful per federal law compliance; bump stocks prohibited
- ***Firearm law uniformity:** preemption law, gun laws uniform; localities may be fined for violations
- ***Right of Self-Defense:** NRA-model castle doctrine, *stand your ground* in public areas
- ***Open carry:** prohibited in all public areas; exceptions for fishing, hunting & camping
- ***Licensed concealed carry:** licenses issued to residents and nonresidents on a "shall issue" basis
- ***Constitutional or "no permit required" concealed carry:** no
- ***Out-of-state permit recognition:** conditional recognition of permits from other states (see p. 65)
- ***Weapons allowed for *licensed* carry:** handguns, knives, stun guns, tear gas guns and billies

VEHICLES

- ***Vehicle carry by non-permittees:** firearms may be concealed and loaded while carried in a private vehicle provided they are "securely encased or otherwise not readily accessible"
- ***Vehicle gun possession at colleges:** lawful for any gun owner at all public universities
- ***Vehicle gun possession at K-12 schools:** firearms prohibited by most local districts
- ***Duty to notify LEO of permit status:** upon demand of police officer
- ***RV carry while "boondocking":** parking lot owners may *not* prohibit guns in vehicles – see p.8

- ***State Parks:** concealed handgun carry by recognized licensees permitted
- ***Restaurants serving alcohol:** permittees may carry while eating in dining areas – see p.3
- ***Hotels:** subject to hotel policy enforcement – see p.7
- ***Airports:** carry prohibited in passenger terminals; car carry in parking lots O.K. – see p.9

Florida's status as a popular vacation destination results in quite a few visitors to the state every year. These people will be pleased to know that Florida's firearms laws are generally favorable for the occasional traveler so long as several important aspects are kept in mind.

Recognized permittees: A license is required to carry a concealed firearm on foot or in a vehicle. The Division of Licensing issues such permits to qualified persons 21 years and older for a seven-year term. These permits allow the carry of handguns, knives, stun guns, tear gas guns and billies.

Florida issues licenses to nonresidents and recognizes permits from states whose laws provide for recognition of Florida permits. Persons with out-of-state permits must have immediate possession of their permits, reside in the state where the permit was issued and be at least 21 years of age. Florida prohibits carry in most universally restricted areas (see p. 7) as well as scholastic and professional athletic events not related to firearms, courthouses, police stations, polling places, meetings of governing bodies, K-12 schools, college campuses, career centers, mental health facilities, airport terminals, bars and places of nuisance (illegal gambling and prostitution houses).

Persons without recognized permits: Carry in a private vehicle is allowed if the firearm is *securely encased* or is *not otherwise readily accessible. Securely encased* includes carry in a snapped holster (off one's person), glove compartment, gun case or a closed box or container. *Not readily accessible* means locked in the trunk of a car or the storage compartment of a pick-up truck or RV. Either of these conditions is legal for non-licensed carry. Carry in a public vehicle, such as a bus, is allowed when the firearm is securely encased and not in the person's manual possession. But firearms concealed *on the person* while occupying any vehicle are illegal. This would include a gun under one's clothing or hidden anywhere on the person.

All Persons: Open carry while on foot is prohibited in all public areas except when one is lawfully hunting, camping or fishing. This prohibition includes licensees and non-licensees. The state also prohibits most businesses from preventing customers or employees from possessing firearms in their locked vehicles while those vehicles are parked on company grounds. Florida's preemption law prevents localities from regulating most aspects of firearm ownership and provides penalties for any locality's willful infringement. With the exception of some zoning laws, firearm regulation is uniform in the state.

Georgia

Total prohibition *(+0, the empire state of South leads the way in good gun laws)* **Total freedom**

0 ------- 10 ------- 20 ------- 30 ------- 40 ------- 50 ------- 60 ------- 70 ------- 80 ------ 90 ------ 100

^

CHECKLIST

***Standard firearms & ammo:** no permit required for possession or sale – see p. 3
***Semi-auto guns & high capacity magazines:** no permit required for possession or sale
***Machine guns & suppressors:** ownership lawful per federal law compliance
***Firearm law uniformity:** preemption law, firearm laws uniform throughout state
***Right of Self-Defense:** NRA-model castle doctrine, *stand your ground* in public areas
***Open carry:** prohibited unless one possesses a recognized license (see exceptions below)
***Licensed concealed carry:** licenses issued on a "shall issue" basis to residents only
***Constitutional or "no permit required" concealed carry:** no
***Out-of-state permit recognition:** conditional recognition of permits from other states (see p. 65)
***Weapons allowed for *licensed* carry:** limited to handguns and knives

VEHICLES

***Vehicle carry by non-permittees:** loaded firearms may be transported anywhere in a private passenger vehicle (see below for details)
***Vehicle gun possession at colleges:** lawful for permittees
***Vehicle gun possession at K-12 schools:** Georgia permittee w/loaded handgun lawful
***Duty to notify LEO of permit/carry status:** upon demand of police officer
***RV carry while "boondocking":** parking lot owners may *not* prohibit guns in vehicles – see p.8

***State Parks:** concealed handgun carry by recognized licensees permitted
***Restaurants serving alcohol:** permittees may carry while eating in dining areas – see p.3
***Hotels:** subject to hotel policy enforcement – see p.7
***Airports:** carry allowed in non-sterile terminal areas and parking lots – see p.9

Despite Atlanta, Georgia still maintains a distinctly rural character for guns. Some cities, such as Kennesaw, even require all citizens to possess at least one firearm in their home for self-defense.

Recognized permittees: The state requires a license to carry a weapon (handgun or knife) on one's person in a concealed or open manner. Georgia issues permits through the probate court of an applicant's home county to qualified persons 21 years or older for five year terms. The state does not issue permits to nonresidents but recognizes permits from states that also recognize Georgia permits as long as the permittee is not a resident of Georgia. Military persons are exempt from needing a license and may use their military IDs as proof of this exemption. Recognized permittees/persons may carry in most public areas except churches (unless allowed by church), school safety zones (K-12 & certain prohibited areas of colleges), courthouses, mental health facilities, businesses that post signs and state & local government buildings with security screenings. Concealed handgun carry is now allowed in many outdoor areas of colleges but remains prohibited for most buildings and athletic facilities. Parking lots for most of the above-named areas are O.K. if the licensee keeps his weapon locked in his vehicle.

Persons without recognized permits: A non-permittee who is not prohibited by law from possessing a handgun may carry a loaded firearm (handgun, rifle or shotgun) anywhere in his *own* vehicle, home or place of business. Someone who qualifies for, but does not possess, a Georgia weapons license (ie. 21 years or older and *not* a felon, illegal drug user or patient at a mental hospital or drug treatment center) may carry a loaded firearm in any vehicle he occupies. While a non-permittee is on foot, he may carry a handgun provided the weapon is unloaded and cased.

Open carry of a loaded handgun is prohibited in most public areas without a recognized license. But hunters and sportsmen may carry loaded handguns on their persons while hunting, fishing or shooting so long as they possesses the necessary state permits for those activities (if such permits are required) and have the permission of the owner upon whose land they operate.

All Persons: Any person who is not prohibited from possessing a firearm may carry a loaded long gun while on foot in most public areas without a permit as long as the gun remains in the "open and fully exposed" to view. Because carry permits only authorize handgun or knife carry, licensees & non-licensees are required to carry their loaded long guns in this manner.

Hawaii

Total prohibition *(-1, permanent move of guns out-of-state requires notification)* **Total freedom**

0 ------- 10 ------- 20 ------- 30 ------- 40 ------- 50 ------- 60 ------- 70 ------- 80 ------ 90 ------ 100

^

CHECKLIST

- ***Standard firearms & ammo:** restricted, registration required within 72 hrs of arrival; ammo must be kept at home unless transported in a closed container to target range, repair place, etc
- ***Semi-auto guns & high capacity magazines:** pistol magazines over 10 shots prohibited; possession of "assault pistols" & bump stocks prohibited
- ***Machine guns & suppressors:** personal ownership prohibited
- ***Firearm law uniformity:** no preemption law, localities may enact their own gun laws
- ***Right of Self-Defense:** no NRA-model castle doctrine, *duty to retreat* in public areas
- ***Open carry:** prohibited in all public areas
- ***Licensed concealed carry:** license issued on a "may issue" basis, valid only in issuing county
- ***Constitutional or "no permit required" concealed carry:** no
- ***Out-of-state permit recognition:** no recognition of out-of-state carry permits
- ***Weapons allowed for *licensed* carry:** limited to handguns only

VEHICLES

- ***Vehicle carry by non-permittees:** firearms generally not allowed in vehicles unless one has a Hawaii permit to carry. (see below for exceptions)
- ***Vehicle gun possession at colleges:** subject to college administrative policy
- ***Vehicle gun possession at K-12 schools:** Hawaii permittee w/loaded handgun lawful
- ***Duty to notify LEO of permit status:** upon demand of police officer
- ***RV carry while "boondocking":** parking lot owners may restrict gun carry by visitors – see p.8
- ***State Parks:** firearms must remain cased, unloaded and stowed in a vehicle
- ***Restaurants serving alcohol:** permittees may carry while eating in dining areas – see p.3
- ***Hotels:** subject to hotel policy enforcement – see p.7
- ***Airports:** carry allowed in non-sterile terminal areas and parking lots – see p.9

Although it is doubtful anyone would ever take a "road trip" to Hawaii (absent construction of a very long bridge), travelers to America's fiftieth state may still find themselves inquiring about state regulation involving the carry and possession of firearms. Hawaii has very strict laws in this area making firearm ownership, especially by non-residents, next to impossible.

Hawaii permittees: Hawaii requires a permit to carry a loaded, concealed handgun on one's person or in a vehicle. Residents and non-residents who are at least 21 years old, U.S. citizens or official representatives of foreign governments may apply to any chief of police for a permit that is valid in that county for a one year term and allows the concealed carry of a handgun only. Hawaii does not recognize permits from other states and operates as a "may issue" domain. Consequently, few permits have been issued in the last thirty years.

Persons without Hawaii permits: It is unlawful to carry firearms or ammunition in a vehicle unless one has a Hawaii permit. A legal exception exists which allows the transport of unloaded and securely cased firearms from the point of purchase to home or from home to a firing range, police station, place of formal hunter/shooter education or repair shop. Ammunition kept in enclosed containers may also be transported within these parameters. Non-residents may have a difficult time fitting into one of these exceptions unless they have relatives living in Hawaii. Concealed or open carry of a firearm by anyone on foot is strictly prohibited unless one is engaged in lawful hunting with a proper permit. A hunter may then carry an unconcealed, loaded pistol as long as that pistol and its ammunition have been approved for hunting in accordance with state statutes.

All Persons: All firearms must be registered with authorities within seventy-two hours of entering the state. Persons possessing these guns must be at least 21. Handguns may not be possessed without first acquiring an approval permit from the police. Shotguns and rifles do not require a possession permit. But registration is still mandatory. Personal ownership of machine guns or any other Class III items is strictly prohibited. Semi-automatic military rifles are currently treated the same as rifles and shotguns with increased regulation a possibility. Assault pistols such as the TEC-9 and M-11 are prohibited along with any high capacity pistol magazine capable of holding more than ten rounds.

Idaho

Total prohibition ***(+5, permitless carry allowed for any U.S. citizen)*** **Total freedom**

0 ------- 10 ------- 20 ------- 30 ------- 40 ------- 50 ------- 60 ------- 70 ------- 80 ------ 90 ------ 100

^

CHECKLIST

- ***Standard firearms & ammo:** no permit required for possession or sale – p.3
- ***Semi-auto guns & high capacity magazines:** no permit required for possession or sale
- ***Machine guns & suppressors:** ownership lawful per federal law compliance
- ***Firearm law uniformity:** preemption law, firearm laws uniform throughout state
- ***Right of Self-Defense:** NRA-model castle doctrine, *stand your ground* in public areas
- ***Open carry:** unrestricted in most public areas and generally accepted
- ***Licensed concealed carry:** licenses issued on a "shall issue" basis to residents and nonresidents
- ***Constitutional or "no permit required" concealed carry:** yes – see below
- ***Out-of-state permit recognition:** automatic recognition of carry permits from all other states
- ***Weapons allowed for *licensed* carry:** include any lawful deadly weapon

VEHICLES

- ***Vehicle carry by non-permittees:** deadly weapons (including loaded handguns, rifles and shotguns) may be carried anywhere in a motor vehicle (per 2019 law change)
- ***Vehicle gun possession at colleges:** lawful for ID enhanced permittees & retired LEOs
- ***Vehicle gun possession at K-12 schools:** Idaho permittee w/loaded handgun lawful
- ***Duty to notify LEO of permit/carry status:** upon demand of police officer
- ***RV carry while "boondocking":** parking lot owners may restrict gun carry by visitors – see p.8

- ***State Parks:** concealed handgun carry by recognized licensees permitted
- ***Restaurants serving alcohol:** permittees may carry while eating in dining areas – see p.3
- ***Hotels:** statutory allowance for guest rejection or ejectment for gun possession – see p.7
- ***Airports:** carry allowed in non-sterile terminal areas and parking lots – see p.9

Idaho's frontier heritage and "permitless carry" for any U.S. citizen provides the traveler with a gun-friendly environment while exploring the state's northern panhandle. In Idaho, firearms are much like potatoes. Both are essential to defining the state's classic character.

Recognized permittees: Idaho will issue both regular & enhanced concealed weapon permits through any county sheriff to qualified persons 21 years or older for 5 year terms. A non-resident must have a carry license from his home state to apply for the "enhanced" permit. These licenses (both regular & enhanced) allow the carry of most lawful deadly weapons. 18-20 year olds may apply for provisional permits that renew as enhanced permits. Idaho will issue permits to nonresidents as well as recognize any permit issued by another state.

Persons without recognized permits: Idaho allows the concealed carry of a deadly weapon without a license by any U.S. citizen who is over the age of 18 and would otherwise be eligible for a license (ie. no intervening legal issues like prior felony convictions). On foot, carry is allowed anywhere except the restricted areas enumerated in the "All persons" section below. In a vehicle, weapons may be concealed or carried openly anywhere including under the seat, the vehicle's dash, glove compartment, console box or trunk.

All Persons: Idaho's "permitless concealed carry" does not affect other aspects of the state's gun laws. Open carry is still lawful throughout the state for those 18 or older. And everyone is still barred from carrying in jails, courthouses, K-12 schools and private businesses that post against carry. State universities may prohibit carry on their campuses through rules set forth by the colleges' governing boards. But Idaho exempts enhanced permittees and retired LEOs from these regulations. Retired LEOs may carry just about anywhere on a campus while "enhanced" permittees are limited to outdoor areas. Indoor areas such as dormitories and entertainment facilities would still be off-limits unless one was a retired LEO certified for carry.

Idaho prevents localities from regulating most aspects of firearms ownership. But parking lot protections only extend to limiting employer liability. Lots may still be posted against gun possession and carry.

Illinois

Total prohibition *(+1, Idaho & Nevada residents may apply for IL permits)* **Total freedom**

0 ------- 10 ------- 20 ------- 30 ------- 40 ------- 50 ------- 60 ------- 70 ------- 80 ------ 90 ------ 100

^ (70)

CHECKLIST

- ***Standard firearms & ammo:** restricted, firearm identification card required for residents
- ***Semi-auto guns & high capacity magazines:** firearm identification card required for residents; local restrictions on assault rifles and high capacity magazines possible
- ***Machine guns or suppressors:** personal ownership prohibited
- ***Firearm law uniformity:** preemption law, handgun regulation preempted; ordinances regulating long guns, "assault rifles" & laser sights still exist in some cities
- ***Right of Self-Defense:** no NRA castle doctrine, *stand your ground* in public not codified
- ***Open carry:** prohibited in all public areas
- ***Licensed concealed carry:** licenses issued on a "shall issue" basis to residents and nonresidents
- ***Constitutional or "no permit required" concealed carry:** no
- ***Out-of-state permit recognition:** no recognition of out-of-state carry permits
- ***Weapons allowed for *licensed* carry:** limited to handguns only

VEHICLES

- ***Vehicle carry by non-residents:** any nonresident who has a carry permit issued by his home state may carry a loaded handgun in his vehicle; long guns must remain unloaded and cased if the possessor has a carry permit or a FOID card; if the nonresident lacks a permit, he must also stow any firearms or ammo in the trunk in an unloaded and cased condition
- ***Vehicle gun possession at colleges:** lawful for permittees, but subject to college policy
- ***Vehicle gun possession at K-12 schools:** Illinois permittee w/loaded handgun lawful
- ***Duty to notify LEO of permit status:** upon demand of police officer
- ***RV carry while "boondocking":** some exemptions for permittees, but lot postings still exist: p.8

- ***State Parks:** concealed handgun carry by Illinois licensees permitted in most outdoor areas
- ***Restaurants serving alcohol:** permittees may carry while eating in dining areas – p.3
- ***Hotels:** subject to hotel policy enforcement & "force of law" posting prohibitions – see p.7
- ***Airports:** carry prohibited on all property; car carry O.K. if gun is in closed compartment of locked car

Illinois finally joined the ranks of the nation's 49 other states by enacting a concealed carry law. And despite numerous restrictions on where one can carry, the law and accompanying preemption statute are marked improvements over what had been a "no public carry" norm in the "Land of Lincoln."

Illinois permittees: A license is required to carry a loaded handgun concealed on or about ones person in public or in a vehicle. The Illinois State Police will issue such a license for a 5-year term to a qualified person who is 21 years or older. Illinois does not recognize out-of-state permits, but will issue permits to nonresidents from Arkansas, Idaho, Mississippi, Nevada, Texas and Virginia for a $300.00 fee.

An Illinois permittee is quite limited as to where he can carry. Prohibited areas include childcare facilities, govt. buildings (including rest areas), courts, schools, hospitals, nursing homes, buses & trains, bars, permitted public gatherings, special events serving alcohol, playgrounds, local parks & athletic areas, colleges, casinos, stadiums, amusement parks, airports, libraries, museums, zoos & private properties that prohibit carry. All these areas must post signs alerting visitors to the prohibitions. And permittees are allowed to keep their concealed handguns in the trunk or glove compartment of their locked vehicles while in the parking lots of these areas.

Non-residents: A non-resident who can legally carry a firearm in public in his home state may carry a concealed, loaded handgun in his vehicle. This would include the passenger compartment of a car or the lockable container of a motorcycle. This exception only applies to nonresidents and is practically limited to those with carry permits from their home states. If the non-resident leaves his car, it must be locked and the handgun stored in a closed compartment.

All Persons: Long guns in a vehicle must remain cased and unloaded regardless of permit status. If a nonresident lacks a valid permit, he must also stow these weapons and any ammo in the trunk. Illinois prohibits open carry and allows some localities to ban assault weapon possession. And even though all regulation of handgun-related issues is preempted by the state, some cities, such as Chicago, Thornton & Cicero are still enforcing ordinances prohibiting possession of laser sights.

Indiana

Total prohibition *(+1, A.G. opinion confirms that cities may not infringe on gun rights)* **Total freedom**

0 ------- 10 ------- 20 ------- 30 ------- 40 ------- 50 ------- 60 ------- 70 ------- 80 ------ 90 ------ 100

^

CHECKLIST

***Standard firearms & ammo:** no permit required for possession or sale – see p.3
***Semi-auto guns & high capacity magazines:** no permit required for possession or sale
***Machine guns & suppressors:** ownership lawful per federal law compliance
***Firearm law uniformity:** preemption law, gun laws uniform; localities may be sued for violations
***Right of Self-Defense:** NRA-model castle doctrine, *stand your ground* in public areas
***Open carry:** prohibited unless one possesses a recognized permit
***Licensed concealed carry:** licenses issued on a "shall issue" basis to residents and nonresidents
***Constitutional or "no permit required" concealed carry:** no
***Out-of-state permit recognition:** automatic recognition for nonresidents with carry permits
***Weapons allowed for *licensed* carry:** limited to handguns only

VEHICLES

***Vehicle carry by non-permittees:** handguns must be unloaded, cased and stowed in the trunk or rear storage area; loaded rifles and shotguns may be carried in the passenger compartment but should be secured in cases (see "all persons" below)
***Vehicle gun possession at colleges:** subject to college administrative policy
***Vehicle gun possession at K-12 schools:** Indiana permittee w/loaded handgun lawful
***Duty to notify LEO of permit status:** upon demand of police officer
***RV carry while "boondocking":** parking lot owners may restrict gun carry by visitors – see p.8

***State Parks:** concealed handgun carry by recognized licensees permitted
***Restaurants serving alcohol:** permittees may carry while eating in dining areas – see p.3
***Hotels:** subject to hotel policy enforcement – see p.7
***Airports:** carry allowed in non-sterile terminal areas and parking lots – see p.9

Indiana has one of America's oldest "shall issue" carry laws. Since 1935, Indiana has allowed residents and nonresidents with regular places of employment or business in the state to obtain licenses to carry loaded handguns for personal protection.

Recognized permittees: Indiana issues licenses that are valid for five years, cost less than $50.00 and allow both concealed and open carry. Residents, and non-residents who work in Indiana, are eligible. Residents may also apply for more expensive lifetime carry licenses. Such permits are valid for the applicant's life. Nonresidents with out-of-state permits are granted automatic recognition for handgun carry but must comply with whatever restrictions exist on their out-of-state permits. For example, if the permit requires the handgun to remain concealed, then it must remain concealed even though Indiana law allows open carry with a permit.

Recognized permittees may carry their loaded handguns in most public areas. Some notable exceptions would be riverboat casinos, K-12 schools (unless attending worship service at a church located on school property) and the state fair. These areas are off-limits unless the licensee leaves his gun stored out of sight in the glove compartment or trunk of his locked vehicle. The Indiana government center, horse race tracks and Falls of the Ohio state park are also off-limits, with no allowances for car carry.

Indiana's preemption law makes local regulation of licensees virtually non-existent. Localities may still prohibit carry in courthouses, hospitals and some special events. But attempting regulation anywhere else could result in stiff legal sanctions against the locality.

Persons without recognized permits: Vehicle carry of a handgun is prohibited unless the weapon is securely cased and unloaded so as not to be readily accessible for immediate use. Stowage in the trunk or rear most portion of an SUV or RV would satisfy this requirement. Open or concealed carry of loaded handguns by unlicensed persons is generally not allowed in Indiana unless the person is engaged in legal hunting activity, shooting at a target range or attending a firearms instructional course.

All Persons: Vehicle carry of loaded long guns is allowed in most places except property owned by Indiana's Dept. of Nat'l Resources. Long guns should be unloaded and cased on DNR property. Courts have held that pistol grip shotguns with no shoulder stocks are classified as handguns and require a carry permit. And employees of most businesses may keep firearms in their vehicles while parked on company property.

Iowa

Total prohibition *(+2, range protection and strengthened preemption law)* **Total freedom**

0 ------- 10 ------- 20 ------- 30 ------- 40 ------- 50 ------- 60 ------- 70 ------- 80 ------ 90 ------ 100

^

CHECKLIST

***Standard firearms & ammo:** no restrictions on possession; handgun sales require permit
***Semi-auto guns & high capacity magazines:** no permit required for possession or sale
***Machine guns & suppressors:** machine gun ownership prohibited; suppressor ownership OK
***Firearm law uniformity:** preemption law, gun laws uniform; localities may be sued for violations
***Right of Self-Defense:** NRA-model castle doctrine, *stand your ground* in public areas
***Open carry:** generally prohibited unless one possesses a recognized permit to carry
***Licensed concealed carry:** licenses issued by sheriffs on a "shall issue" basis to residents only; "professional"permits issued to non-residents through Dept.of Public Safety
***Constitutional or "no permit required" concealed carry:** no
***Out-of-state permit recognition:** automatic recognition for all nonresidents with carry permits
***Weapons allowed for *licensed* carry:** any rifle, shotgun, handgun, knife, taser or stun gun

VEHICLES

***Vehicle carry by non-permittees:** handguns may not be carried in a loaded or accessible condition; long guns must be unloaded and cased yet may be accessible to passengers
***Vehicle gun possession at colleges:** prohibited by law
***Vehicle gun possession at K-12 schools:** firearms generally prohibited, except unloaded handgun may be stowed in locked container of passenger compartment or trunk
***Duty to notify LEO of permit status:** upon demand of police officer
***RV carry while "boondocking":** parking lot owners may restrict gun carry by visitors – see p.8

***State Parks:** concealed handgun carry by recognized licensees permitted
***Restaurants serving alcohol:** permittees may carry while eating in dining areas – see p.3
***Hotels:** statutory allowance for guest rejection or ejectment for gun possession – see p.7
***Airports:** carry allowed in non-sterile terminal areas and parking lots – see p.9

Iowa provides out-of-state permittees with ample opportunities for carry options while visiting the state. And while treatment of non-permittees may be stricter than other "bread basket" states of the Midwest, handgun carry for recognized permittees is hassle-free.

Recognized permittees: A license is required to carry a loaded firearm in a vehicle or on one's person while on foot. The state issues professional & non-professional licenses. Non-professional licenses are granted through the sheriff of one's home county to any qualified resident who is at least 21 years old. The licenses are valid for 5 years and allow open or concealed carry of any firearm in most public areas. Notable exceptions include casinos, the state fair, courthouses and state universities. *Concealed*, but not openly displayed, handguns are allowed at the State Capitol. And any open or concealed handgun carry is permitted while operating ATVs & snowmobiles.

Professional licenses are granted to residents through their local sheriff and to non-residents through the Department of Public Safety. The professional licenses are available to anyone 18 years or older whose need to go armed arises out of their employment. Iowa recognizes any valid, out-of-state carry permit so long as the permittee is not a resident of Iowa.

Persons without recognized permits: Handguns in a vehicle must be unloaded and contained inside a closed or fastened container that is too large to conceal on one's person. They may also be transported in a cargo or luggage area where the weapons are inaccessible to the vehicle's occupants. Long guns may remain accessible to passengers if the weapons are unloaded and cased.

Handguns may not be carried on one's person, either concealed or openly, within any municipal limits without a recognized permit. An exception exists which allows persons on recognized target ranges or hunting preserves to carry openly as long as they have the permission of the owner. But public carry of a loaded handgun is generally not allowed without a permit.

All Persons: Iowa prohibits the possession of machine guns, short-barreled rifles and shotguns. The only exception would be for historical reenactors who use firearms classified as "curios and relics." The weapons must also be rendered inoperable before entering the state.

Kansas

Total prohibition *(+0, jayhawkers set the bar for good gun laws in the Midwest)* **Total freedom**

0 ------- 10 ------- 20 ------- 30 ------- 40 ------- 50 ------- 60 ------- 70 ------- 80 ------ 90 ------ 100

^

CHECKLIST

***Standard firearms & ammo:** no permit required for possession or sale – see p. 3
***Semi-auto guns & high capacity magazines:** no permit required for possession or sale
***Machine guns & suppressors:** ownership lawful per federal law compliance
***Firearm law uniformity:** preemption law, firearm laws uniform throughout state
***Right of Self-Defense:** NRA-model castle doctrine, *stand your ground* in public areas
***Open carry:** unrestricted under state law; localities may still prohibit carry in certain bldgs.
***Licensed concealed carry:** licenses issued by A.G. to residents on a "shall issue" basis
***Constitutional or "no permit required" concealed carry:** yes - see below
***Out-of-state permit recognition:** automatic recognition of carry permits from all other states
***Weapons allowed for *licensed* carry:** limited to handguns only

VEHICLES

***Vehicle carry by non-permittees:** loaded firearms may be carried anywhere in a vehicle by law-abiding persons 21 years and older
***Vehicle gun possession at colleges:** handgun possession lawful for any gun owner
***Vehicle gun possession at K-12 schools:** Kansas permittee w/loaded handgun lawful
***Duty to notify LEO of permit/carry status:** upon demand of police officer
***RV carry while "boondocking":** parking lot owners may *not* prohibit guns in vehicles – see p.8

***State Parks:** concealed handgun carry by citizens 21 years and older lawful
***Restaurants serving alcohol:** concealed carry O.K. if premises are not "posted" – see p.3
***Hotels:** subject to hotel policy enforcement – see p.7
***Airports:** carry allowed in non-sterile terminal areas and parking lots – see p.9

In 1892, citizens used their private arms to defeat the Dalton Gang's attack on several banks in downtown Coffeyville. While exemplifying the best in Western self-reliance, this incident also explains why jayhawkers sport some of the best gun laws in the nation. Firearms have always had a positive impact in the state. And gun-owning travelers will find this mindset quite refreshing.

Recognized permittees: The attorney general issues concealed carry licenses for four-year terms to residents who are at least 21 years old. Even though no longer required for concealed carry in Kansas, these licenses allow residents to enjoy reciprocity while traveling to other states. All out-of-state permittees are likewise granted recognition in Kansas as long as they are at least 21 years old.

Prohibited places can include any private or public building that chooses to restrict carry. But the buildings *must* be posted with A.G. approved signage or, in certain instances, provide adequate security screenings for the prohibitions to be enforceable. State facilities may also regulate the manner of carry (ie. handguns must be holstered, etc.). But only the buildings, and not the parking lots, of these areas are subject to prohibitions or regulatory actions. Handguns kept in locked vehicles are lawful. And violations of carry restrictions in posted buildings are generally not considered criminal offenses.

Persons without recognized permits: Kansas no longer requires a license to carry a concealed firearm. A non-permittee who is 21 years or older may carry a loaded gun anywhere in his vehicle. Kansas' preemption law ensures no local regulation of this right.

Open or concealed carry of a handgun while on foot is allowed in most public areas for those 21 and older. Hunters and fisherman are even granted statutory protection for carry while engaged in their pursuits. And most local ordinances regulating this have been eliminated. But property owners (both private and govt.) may still prohibit carry within their buildings by posting signs.

All Persons: All gun carriers should be aware that some prohibited areas, such as the state capitol and state offices, only allow carry of *concealed* handguns. And universities may even require chambers of guns to remain unloaded while visiting campus. Tribal lands (casinos, etc.) generally recognize licensees but may not extend the same courtesies to non-licensees. Rules vary by reservation.

Kentucky

Total prohibition ***(+0, highest per capita gun ownership – need we say more!)*** **Total freedom**

0 ------- 10 ------- 20 ------- 30 ------- 40 ------- 50 ------- 60 ------- 70 ------- 80 ------ 90 ------ 100

^

CHECKLIST

***Standard firearms & ammo:** no permit required for possession or sale – see p.3
***Semi-auto guns & high capacity magazines:** no permit required for possession or sale
***Machine guns & suppressors:** ownership lawful per federal law compliance
***Firearm law uniformity:** preemption law, gun laws uniform; localities may be sued for violations
***Right of Self-Defense:** NRA-model castle doctrine, *stand your ground* in public areas
***Open carry:** unrestricted in most public areas and generally accepted
***Licensed concealed carry:** licenses issued by state police to residents on a "shall issue" basis
***Constitutional or "no permit required" concealed carry:** yes – see below
***Out-of-state permit recognition:** automatic recognition for all non-residents with carry permits
***Weapons allowed for *licensed* carry:** include any lawful deadly weapon

VEHICLES

***Vehicle carry by non-permittees:** loaded firearms may be carried anywhere in a vehicle
***Vehicle gun possession at colleges:** lawful for any gun owner
***Vehicle gun possession at K-12 schools:** Kentucky permittee w/loaded handgun lawful (permittee must be a non-student)
***Duty to notify LEO of permit/carry status:** upon demand of police officer
***RV carry while "boondocking":** parking lot owners may *not* prohibit guns in vehicles – see p.8

***State Parks:** concealed handgun carry by recognized licensees permitted
***Restaurants serving alcohol:** permittees may carry while eating in dining areas – see p.3
***Hotels:** subject to hotel policy enforcement – see p.7
***Airports:** carry allowed in non-sterile terminal areas and parking lots – see p.9

One of America's greatest statesmen was Kentucky's own Henry Clay. Famous for arranging deals that delayed the inevitable conflict between North and South, he was known as the nation's "great compromiser." While still revered in the Bluegrass, his penchant for compromise would be in stark contrast to those tasked with crafting the state's gun laws. When it comes to guns rights in Kentucky, there is no compromise.

Recognized permittees: Kentucky's State Police issue licenses to carry concealed firearms, or other deadly weapons, through the sheriff of an applicant's home county for five-year terms. Kentucky does not grant permits to nonresidents but will recognize any permit issued by another state as long as the permittee is not a resident of Kentucky. A recognized permittee may carry concealed in most public areas. Prohibited places include childcare centers, K-12 schools, bars, legislative meetings, law enforcement offices, and courthouses. Colleges, hospitals, local governments, and private businesses may also ban carry in their buildings by posting signs. But prohibitions in these areas are not criminal offenses.

Persons without recognized permits: Kentucky no longer requires a license to carry a firearm concealed. In 2019, the legislature enacted constitutional or "permitless" carry. Loaded firearms may now be carried anywhere in a vehicle. Hidden from view in a console box, glove compartment or under the seat or visibly displayed in a belt holster are all lawful carry modes for those without permits.

On foot, permitless concealed carry is allowed in most places where licensed carry is permitted. Permitless carriers must still abide by the same place restrictions noted above for licensees. And carry in your vehicle on K-12 school grounds would require a Kentucky-issued license to avoid running afoul of federal school zone restrictions (see p. 4).

Open carry of a firearm while on foot is also allowed in most public areas. Such carry is best limited to visible belt holsters secured on one's hip. Kentucky's strong preemption law now provides stiff penalties for any locality that attempts to regulate this activity.

All Persons: A property owner may not prohibit employees and customers from carrying firearms in their vehicles while the vehicles are parked on that owner's property. Civil penalties exist for property owners who violate this mandate. Also, game wardens may not harass any sportsmen who carry firearms for self-defense while hunting or fishing.

Louisiana

Total prohibition *(+3, enhanced preemption & limited church carry)* **Total freedom**

0 ------- 10 ------- 20 ------- 30 ------- 40 ------- 50 ------- 60 ------- 70 ------- 80 ------ 90 ------ 100

^

CHECKLIST

***Standard firearms & ammo:** no permit required for possession or sale – see p. 3

***Semi-auto guns & high capacity magazines:** no permit required for possession or sale

***Machine guns & suppressors:** ownership restricted to "war relic" machine guns; suppressor ownership lawful per federal law compliance

***Firearm law uniformity:** preemption law, localities prohibited from enacting any ordinances after 1985 that regulate firearms

***Right of Self-Defense:** NRA-model castle doctrine, *stand your ground* in public areas

***Open carry:** unrestricted in most public areas and generally accepted

***Licensed concealed carry:** licenses issued by state police to residents on a "shall issue" basis

***Constitutional or "no permit required" concealed carry:** no

***Out-of-state permit recognition:** conditional recognition of permits from other states (see p. 65)

***Weapons allowed for *licensed* carry:** limited to handguns only

VEHICLES

***Vehicle carry by non-permittees:** loaded firearms may be carried openly or in the glove compartment, console box, or trunk of vehicle

***Vehicle gun possession at colleges:** lawful for any gun owner

***Vehicle gun possession at K-12 schools:** Louisiana permittee w/loaded handgun lawful

***Duty to notify LEO of permit status:** immediately upon official contact

***RV carry while "boondocking":** parking lot owners may *not* prohibit guns in vehicles – see p. 8

***State Parks:** concealed handgun carry by recognized licensees permitted

***Restaurant serving alcohol:** permittees may carry while eating in dining areas – see p.3

***Hotels:** subject to hotel policy enforcement & possible "force of law" posting prohibitions – see p.7

***Airports:** carry allowed in non-sterile terminal areas and parking lots -- see p.9

Louisiana is called "The Sportsman's Paradise" for its vast network of game preserves. This condition, along with the state's political conservatism, ensures a pleasant visit for the gun-owning traveler.

Recognized permittees: Louisiana requires a license to carry a handgun concealed upon one's person. Such permits are issued by the Department of Public Safety to qualified residents who are 21 or older for five years or a lifetime, depending upon the choice of the applicant. Louisiana does not grant permits to nonresidents but will recognize licenses issued by states whose laws also recognize Louisiana permits. Recognized permittees must be at least 21 years old and may not be Louisiana residents. Permittees may carry in most public areas except police stations, jails, courthouses, polling places, parades, K-12 schools, the state capitol, public buildings used as meeting places for a governing authority, bars, and many parts of college campuses. Church carry is now O.K. if the church leader grants permission. And permittees must declare their identity to police when approached.

Persons without recognized permits: A loaded handgun may be carried almost anywhere in a vehicle. Glove compartments, console boxes, or seat pockets are all legitimate placement areas. Plain view carry in a snapped holster or other similar carry rig is also acceptable as long as one's clothing does not cover the gun.

Loaded rifles and shotguns may be carried in commercial gun cases, gun racks or outside storage compartments. The state only restricts weapons that are concealed *on one's person.* This prohibition would include firearms hidden under one's shirt, jacket or outer garment as well as weapons contained within any purse or briefcase carried by a person.

A handgun may be carried openly while on foot in most public areas. The weapon should be exposed to view. And placement in a snapped belt holster is recommended.

All Persons: Louisiana's preemption law prevents localities from regulating most aspects of firearm possession, carry and transport. But while cities were recently prohibited from restricting carry in public buildings and commercial establishments, some ordinances enacted before July, 1985 may still exist.

Vehicle carry on most public and private parking lots is protected activity. Property owners may not prohibit visitors from having firearms in their vehicles while parked on the owners' lots.

Maine

Total prohibition (*+0, New England's back country rivals Alaska for good gun laws!*) **Total freedom**

0 ------- 10 ------- 20 ------- 30 ------- 40 ------- 50 ------- 60 ------- 70 ------- 80 ------ 90 ------ 100

^

CHECKLIST

- ***Standard firearms & ammo:** no permit required for possession or sale – see p. 3
- ***Semi-auto guns & high capacity magazines:** no permit required for possession or sale
- ***Machine guns & suppressors:** ownership lawful per federal law compliance
- ***Firearm law uniformity:** preemption law, firearm laws uniform throughout state
- ***Open carry:** unrestricted under state law in most public areas; some exceptions – see below
- ***Right of Self-Defense:** no NRA-model castle doctrine, *duty to retreat* in public areas
- ***Licensed concealed carry:** licenses issued on a "shall issue" basis to residents and nonresidents
- ***Constitutional or "no permit required" concealed carry:** yes – see below
- ***Out-of-state permit recognition:** conditional recognition of permits from other states (see p.65)
- ***Weapons allowed for *licensed* carry:** limited to handguns only

VEHICLES

- ***Vehicle carry by non-permittees:** anyone 21 years or older may carry a loaded handgun anywhere in a vehicle; long guns must remain unloaded and may be secured in commercial gun cases or stowed in the trunk
- ***Vehicle gun possession at colleges:** subject to college administrative policy
- ***Vehicle gun possession at K-12 schools:** firearm possession prohibited
- ***Duty to notify LEO of permit/carry status:** upon demand for permittees only (see below)
- ***RV carry while "boondocking":** parking lot owners may restrict gun carry by visitors – see p.8

- ***State Parks:** concealed handgun carry by recognized licensees permitted (except Baxter S.P.)
- ***Restaurants serving alcohol:** concealed carry O.K. if premises are not "posted" – see p.3
- ***Hotels:** statutory allowance for guest rejection & "force of law" posting prohibitions – see p.7
- ***Airports:** carry allowed in non-sterile terminal areas and parking lots of most airports (Augusta state airport prohibits carry on its grounds through administrative rule) – see p.9

Maine is well known for its "back country" reputation. The state will provide some beautiful scenery as well as a friendly atmosphere for gun owners. Maine's enactment of a law allowing concealed carry without a permit makes the Pine Tree State one of our nation's best.

Recognized permittees: Despite constitutional carry, Maine will still issue a license to carry a loaded handgun in a vehicle or concealed about one's person to anyone 18 years or older for a four year term. Residents apply to their local police chief while nonresidents apply directly to the State Police. Most find the licenses helpful in enhancing reciprocity options. Maine will recognize licenses from residents of states that also honor Maine's permits. Recognized permittees may carry concealed, loaded handguns throughout the state. But casinos, courthouses, restaurants serving alcohol that post against carry, K-12 schools, private property w/postings, wildlife sanctuaries, labor disputes and most of the state capitol are off-limits to all gun carry. And permittees who carry in Acadia National Park and most state parks must keep their handguns concealed. Baxter State Park prohibits anyone from carrying a firearm.

Persons without recognized permits: Any person who is 21 years or older may carry a loaded handgun anywhere in his vehicle. Glove compartments, console boxes, under one's seat, or on one's person are all legitimate. Any active duty military with official I.D. between the ages of 18-21 may also carry.

While on foot, anyone may openly carry a loaded handgun. And those 21 years and older (and military personnel) may carry concealed handguns (but no other weapons) without a permit. Maine requires these non-permittees to immediately inform a police officer upon official contact that they have a concealed handgun. Those with permits do not have this requirement.

In addition to the areas prohibited to licensees, those who carry without permits are also barred from carry in Acadia National Park and all state parks. These places (except Baxter – see above) require those carrying handguns to possess licenses. Non-permitted carry is not allowed.

All Persons: Maine forbids the carry of any *loaded* long gun in a vehicle. This means that *everyone,* even those with permits, must keep rifles & shotguns unloaded. Magazines may be loaded but may not be attached to, or inserted in, any of the guns.

Maryland

Total prohibition ***(+0, Baltimore politics make it a nightmare for gun owners)*** **Total freedom**

0 ------- 10 ------- 20 ------- 30 ------- 40 ------- 50 ------- 60 ------- 70 ------- 80 ------ 90 ------ 100

^ (about 20)

CHECKLIST

***Standard firearms & ammo:** no restrictions on possession; handgun sales require permit - see p.3

***Semi-auto guns & high capacity magazines:** import of *assault weapons* prohibited; transfer or sale of over 10 shot magazines prohibited; bump stocks prohibited

***Machine guns & suppressors:** state registration required of machine guns; suppressor ownership lawful per federal law compliance

***Firearm law uniformity:** preemption law with notable exceptions, see below

***Right of Self-Defense:** no NRA-model castle doctrine, *duty to retreat* in public areas

***Open carry:** prohibited in all public areas unless one possesses a Maryland permit

***Licensed concealed carry:** licenses issued on a "may issue" basis to residents and nonresidents

***Constitutional or "no permit required" concealed carry:** no

***Out-of-state permit recognition:** no recognition of out-of-state carry permits

***Weapons allowed for *licensed* carry:** generally limited to handguns and knives

VEHICLES

***Vehicle carry for non-permittees:** loaded, readily accessible handguns prohibited; exceptions exist for unloaded transport; rifles & shotguns must remain unloaded

***Vehicle gun possession at colleges:** subject to college administrative policy

***Vehicle gun possession at K-12 schools:** firearm possession prohibited

***Duty to notify LEO of permit status:** upon demand of police officer

***RV carry while "boondocking":** parking lot owners may restrict gun carry by visitors – see p.8

***State Parks:** possession and carry of firearms prohibited except at designated ranges

***Restaurants serving alcohol:** permittees may carry while eating in dining areas – see p.3

***Hotels:** statutory allowance for guest rejection or ejectment for gun possession – see p.7

***Airports:** carry allowed in non-sterile terminal areas and parking lots (some local postings possible)

Maryland has many restrictions on the sale & importation of handguns and military pattern semi-autos (assault weapons). Handgun purchasers must be licensed. Any firearm classified as an "assault weapon" is banned from import entirely. And the sale or transfer of any over 10 shot magazine is prohibited. Handgun carry is similarly regulated so that unlicensed carry is next to impossible.

Maryland permittees: The state requires a license to carry a loaded handgun on one's person or in a vehicle. The state police issue such permits on a highly discretionary basis to persons demonstrating a *compelling need* for a 2-year term. Maryland will issue permits to nonresidents on rare occasions. But the state will not recognize carry permits from other states. Permittees are prohibited from carrying on K-12 public school property, at public demonstrations, legislative bldgs., some hotels, state-owned public buildings, highway rest areas, most child care centers, state forest & park lands and adult rehabilitation centers.

Persons without Maryland permits: A non-permittee may not carry a handgun on foot or in a vehicle in a loaded or readily accessible manner. But he may transport an unloaded handgun in a secure case if he is traveling to or from a sport shooting event, gun show, hunting, target practice, repair shop or place of purchase. Magazines may remain loaded while in a vehicle as long as they are separate from any handgun.

Travelers *passing through* the state may transport inaccessible handguns even if they are not traveling to one of these events. The guns must be unloaded, cased and, either stowed in the trunk, or locked in a case if the vehicle has no trunk. Ammunition should be in separate cases.

All Persons: Rifles and shotguns may be transported in a vehicle for any reason. But the weapons must be unloaded and secured in commercial cases or gun racks regardless of whether one has a Maryland permit.

Despite a preemption statute, localities may still regulate the discharge of guns within their limits and the carry of firearms within 100 yards of schools, parks, churches, public buildings, and places of public assembly. These local restrictions, coupled with state prohibitions, make carry in Maryland problematic at best.

Massachusetts

Total prohibition *(+0, the Sons of Liberty wouldn't recognize this place)* **Total freedom**

0 ------- 10 ------- 20 ------- 30 ------- 40 ------- 50 ------- 60 ------- 70 ------- 80 ------ 90 ------ 100

^ (10)

CHECKLIST

- ***Standard firearms & ammo:** restricted, Firearm Identification Card required to possess
- ***Semi-auto & high capacity magazines:** restricted, permit required to possess (any assault weapon or over 10 shot mag. made after 9/13/1994 is prohibited); bump stocks banned
- ***Machine guns & suppressors:** restricted, state permit required & federal compliance for machine guns; personal ownership of suppressors prohibited
- ***Firearm law uniformity:** firearm laws are uniformly strict throughout the state
- ***Right of Self-Defense:** no NRA-model castle doctrine, *duty to retreat* in public areas
- ***Open carry:** prohibited in all public areas unless one possesses a Massachusetts permit
- ***Licensed concealed carry:** licenses issued on a "may issue" basis to residents and nonresidents
- ***Constitutional or "no permit required" concealed carry:** no
- ***Out-of-state permit recognition:** no *general* recognition of out-of-state carry permits
- ***Weapons allowed for *licensed* carry:** include handguns and certain rifles and shotguns

VEHICLES

- ***Vehicle carry by non-permittees:** handgun carry generally prohibited; standard rifles and shotguns must be unloaded and securely cased
- ***Vehicle gun possession at colleges:** prohibited by law
- ***Vehicle gun possession at K-12 schools:** firearm possession prohibited
- ***Duty to notify LEO of permit status:** upon demand of police officer
- ***RV carry while "boondocking":** parking lot owners may restrict gun carry by visitors – see p.8

- ***State Parks:** concealed handgun carry by Massachusetts licensees permitted
- ***Restaurants serving alcohol:** permittees may carry while eating in dining areas – see p.3
- ***Hotels:** subject to hotel policy enforcement – see p.7
- ***Airports:** carry prohibited in terminal areas & parking lots of most airports (security zone enforcement)

Unfortunately for gun owners, Massachusetts reflects Ted Kennedy's politics when it comes to laws regulating firearms. Mere possession of rifles, shotguns, handguns and ammunition requires a firearm identification card. And any violation of a Massachusetts' firearm law could carry a minimum sentence of one year in prison for the violator.

Massachusetts permittees: A permit is needed to carry a concealed handgun in your vehicle or on your person while on foot. Such licenses are issued to Massachusetts' residents who are 21 or older for 6-year terms on a highly discretionary basis. The state will issue temporary licenses to carry handguns to nonresidents who have carry permits from their home states. These permits cost $100.00, are valid for one year and may be obtained through the Firearms Records Bureau (617-660-4782). Any permittee in a vehicle must carry his handgun so that it is under his "exclusive" control and not in the possession of a non-permitted passenger.

Massachusetts will only recognize the carry permits of other states if the issuing state has criteria for issuance that are in accordance with Massachusetts' standards. The permittee must also be traveling to a recognized firearm competition or engaged in lawful hunting with a state hunting license. Massachusetts does not publish a list of states that they recognize in this regard.

Persons without Massachusetts permits: Vehicle carry of a handgun without a Massachusetts carry license is prohibited. Handguns may only be transported by travelers who are "passing through" the state under the provisions of McClure-Volkmer (see p 5.)

Nonresidents traveling into or through the state may transport standard rifles, shotguns and ammunition in a vehicle if the items are unloaded and cased. Nonresident hunters may also possess rifles and shotguns if they have nonresident hunting licenses. But possession of most "large capacity" rifles & shotguns defined as assault weapons by state authorities requires a temporary license.

All Persons: All semi-automatic "assault weapons" and over 10 shot magazines made after 1994 are permanently banned from entering the state. "Bump stocks" & "trigger cranks" designed to simulate full-auto fire are also prohibited. And any licensee allowed to possess large capacity long guns must have them unloaded and *locked* in cases while in a vehicle.

Michigan

Total prohibition ***(+0, not bad for residents, but travelers w/o permits will find it tough)*** **Total freedom**

0 ------- 10 ------- 20 ------- 30 ------- 40 ------- 50 ------- 60 ------- 70 ------ 80 ------- 90 ------ 100

^

CHECKLIST

***Standard firearms & ammo:** handgun registration required at purchase; no ammo restrictions

***Semi-auto guns & high capacity mags:** folding stock rifles less than 26" require NFA regstr.

***Machine guns & suppressors:** ownership lawful per federal law compliance

***Firearm law uniformity:** preemption law, firearm laws uniform throughout state

***Right of Self-Defense:** NRA model-castle doctrine, *stand your ground* in public areas

***Open carry:** unrestricted under state law, nonresidents must have home state carry permit

***Licensed concealed carry:** licenses issued by county clerks on a "shall issue" basis to residents

***Constitutional or "no permit required" concealed carry:** no

***Out-of-state permit recognition:** automatic recognition for person w/ permit from home state

***Weapons allowed for *licensed* carry:** limited to handguns and stun guns

VEHICLES

***Vehicle carry by non-permittees:** long guns must be transported unloaded and encased or secured in the trunk; a nonresident may not transport a handgun w/o a home state permit

***Vehicle gun possession at colleges:** subject to college administrative policy

***Vehicle gun possession at K-12 schools:** Michigan permittee w/loaded handgun lawful

***Duty to notify LEO of permit status:** immediately upon official contact

***RV carry while "boondocking":** parking lot owners may restrict gun carry by visitors – see p.8

***State Parks:** concealed handgun carry by recognized licensees permitted

***Restaurants serving alcohol:** permittees may carry while eating in dining areas – see p.3

***Hotels:** subject to hotel policy enforcement – see p.7

***Airports:** carry allowed in non-sterile terminal areas and parking lots – see p.9

Michigan's rustic northern regions draw many gun enthusiasts. Unfortunately, Michigan's gun laws for visitors are stricter than one might expect and should cause the unlicensed traveler concern.

Recognized permittees: A license is required to carry a handgun concealed on your person or within your vehicle. The county clerk of an applicant's home county issues such a permit for a five-year term. These licenses are only available to Michigan residents and exempt the holders from having to obtain a purchase permit on subsequent pistol purchases. A permittee may not carry a *concealed*, loaded pistol in K-12 schools, sports arenas, large entertainment facilities, churches, hospitals, bars, casinos, daycare centers and universities. Parking lots of these areas (except casinos) are O.K. for car carry. And open carry by permittees (except casinos) is lawful as well. But colleges may ban car carry in their parking lots through policy enforcement. And K-12 schools *may* attempt bans on open carry by permittees through policy enforcement as well.

Michigan recognizes any out-of-state permittee with a license from his home state. A permittee must be the actual owner of the pistol he carries and immediately disclose to police that he has a carry license when stopped. Licensees may carry their handguns openly or concealed.

Persons without recognized permits: Michigan residents without carry permits may transport handguns for a "lawful purpose" that are securely cased, unloaded and either stored in the trunk or placed in an area that is not readily accessible. "Lawful purpose" includes transport to locations where the pistol may be employed for most recreational endeavors. The pistol's owner must have also registered the pistol with the Michigan State police when he acquired the pistol. This requirement makes it impossible for a nonresident to transport a pistol in Michigan unless he has a carry permit from his home state.

Michigan allows the open carry of a loaded pistol while on foot in most public areas except K-12 schools, banks, churches, courts, theaters, sports arenas, day care centers, hospitals and alcohol-related businesses. Permittees, however, may carry their pistols openly in these areas absent an intervening policy (ie. open carry in courts may be banned by judicial order). A carrier should keep his pistol in a visible holster and not enter a vehicle unless he has a permit. Open carry without a permit is limited to Michigan residents.

All Persons: Long guns in a vehicle must be unloaded and at least one of the following: (1) broken down, (2) enclosed in a case, (3) placed in the trunk or, (4) inaccessible from the vehicle's interior. And, along with areas prohibited by statute, private property owners may ban carry on all property, including parking lots.

Minnesota

Total prohibition *(+0, good state for licensees, nonpemittees still have it rough)* **Total freedom**

0 ------- 10 ------- 20 ------- 30 ------- 40 ------- 50 ------- 60 ------- 70 ------- 80 ------ 90 ------ 100

^

CHECKLIST

*__Standard firearms & ammo:__ no restrictions on possession (handgun sales require permit) see p.3

*__Semi-auto guns & high capacity mags:__ possession O.K..; assault weapon sales require permit

*__Machine guns & suppressors:__ restrictive, only machine-guns which are curio & relics lawful; suppressor ownership lawful per federal law compliance

*__Firearm law uniformity:__ state preemption law, firearm laws uniform throughout state

*__Right of Self-Defense:__ no NRA-model castle doctrine, *duty to retreat* in public areas

*__Open carry:__ prohibited in all public areas unless one possesses a recognized permit

*__Licensed concealed carry:__ licenses issued on a "shall issue" basis to residents and non-residents

*__Constitutional or "no permit required" concealed carry:__ no

*__Out-of-state permit recognition:__ conditional recognition of permits from other states (see p. 65)

*__Weapons allowed for *licensed* carry:__ limited to handguns only

VEHICLES

*__Vehicle carry by non-permittees:__ all firearms must be securely cased and unloaded

*__Vehicle gun possession at colleges:__ lawful for any gun owner (permittee or nonpermittee)

*__Vehicle gun possession at K-12 schools:__ Minnesota permittee w/loaded handgun lawful; permittee may also exit vehicle to retrieve gun from trunk or rear storage area

*__Duty to notify LEO of permit status:__ upon demand of police officer

*__RV carry while "boondocking":__ *most* parking lot owners may *not* prohibit guns in vehicles – p.8

*__State Parks:__ concealed handgun carry by recognized licensees permitted

*__Restaurants serving alcohol:__ permittees may carry while eating in dining areas – see p.3

*__Hotels:__ statutory allowance for guest rejection or ejectment for gun possession – see p. 7

*__Airports:__ carry allowed in non-sterile terminal areas and parking lots – see p.9

Minnesota's numerous restrictions on the purchase and sale of handguns and "assault weapons" should not concern the casual traveler. But persons visiting America's north central region should be aware of certain legal nuances to ensure an uneventful trip.

Recognized permittees: Minnesota requires a license to carry a loaded handgun on one's person or in a vehicle. Permits are granted on a "shall issue" basis to residents and nonresidents who are at least 21 years old. Application is made to the sheriff of the resident's home county. Non-residents may apply to any sheriff in the state. Permits are valid for five years and allow concealed or open carry. Out-of-state permits from states with similar laws are recognized at the discretion of the Dept. of Public Safety. Aside from some universally restricted areas (p.7) such as K-12 schools, childcare facilities and courthouses (prohibited through judicial order), most public venues are open to carry by permittees. But private establishments that post signs and public institutions, such as universities, which enforce policies against carry, are off-limits. Such places can only prohibit carry within buildings and, with the exception of churches, may not ban carry in parking facilities.

Persons without recognized permits: Handguns in a vehicle must be unloaded and fully contained in closed commercial gun cases. The weapons may be transported in either the passenger compartment or trunk but must always remain unloaded and cased.

While on foot, handguns may be transported between one's premises and place of business without a permit. Persons engaged in lawful hunting and target shooting may also carry handguns without permits while engaged in these pursuits. Aside from these few exceptions, loaded handgun carry is limited to permittees only.

All Persons: Rifles and shotguns in a vehicle must be unloaded and secured in commercial gun cases unless stowed in the trunk. Long guns in a vehicle's trunk must be unloaded but need not be cased. This restriction applies to permittees and non-permittees alike because Minnesota's licensing law only allows for *handgun* carry with a permit. Open carry of long guns while on foot is limited to lawful hunting or target shooting pursuits. Any other possession in public requires that the weapons be unloaded and cased.

Mississippi

Total prohibition *(+0, permitless carry & a vibrant gun culture make it one of our best)* **Total freedom**

0 ------- 10 ------- 20 ------- 30 ------- 40 ------- 50 ------- 60 ------- 70 ------- 80 ------ 90 ------ 100

^ (100)

CHECKLIST

- ***Standard firearms & ammo:** no permit required for possession or sale – see p.3
- ***Semi-auto guns & high capacity magazines:** no permit required for possession or sale
- ***Machine guns & suppressors:** ownership lawful per federal law compliance
- ***Firearm law uniformity:** preemption law, but cities may restrict parks & public meetings
- ***Right of Self-Defense:** NRA-model castle doctrine, *stand your ground* in public areas
- ***Open carry:** unrestricted under state law in most public areas (local restrictions possible)
- ***Licensed concealed carry:** licenses issued by DPS on a "shall issue" basis to residents only
- ***Constitutional or "no permit required" concealed carry:** yes – see below
- ***Out-of-state permit recognition:** automatic recognition of carry permits from all other states
- ***Weapons allow for *licensed* carry:** limited to handguns and stun guns

VEHICLES

- ***Vehicle carry by non-permittees:** loaded, concealed handguns may be carried anywhere in a vehicle; long guns should be unloaded during hunting season
- ***Vehicle gun possession at colleges:** lawful for any non-student gun owner (permit or no permit)
- ***Vehicle gun possession at K-12 schools:** Mississippi non-student permittee w/handgun lawful
- ***Duty to notify LEO of permit/carry status:** upon demand of police officer
- ***RV carry while "boondocking":** parking lot owners may *not* prohibit guns in vehicles – see p.8

- ***State Parks:** concealed handgun carry by licensees & those exercising constitutional carry permitted
- ***Restaurants serving alcohol:** permittees may carry while eating in dining areas – see p.3
- ***Hotels:** subject to hotel policy enforcement & "force of law" posting prohibitions – see p.7
- ***Airports:** carry prohibited in terminals except for MS "enhanced" permittees; parking lots O.K. for all

Mississippi's laws showcase a strong tradition of gun ownership. Constitutional carry and an "enhanced" permit option exemplify the state's commitment to excellence.

Recognized permittees: Licenses to carry concealed handguns are still issued to residents for 5-year terms. These permits may be upgraded to "enhanced" status through additional training that allows permittees to carry in all the prohibited areas listed in the next paragraph except jails, police stations, places of nuisance and some "posted" property. Licenses are not issued to nonresidents but all out-of-state permits are recognized as "regular" permits. Permittees may carry openly or concealed.

Carry for "regular" permittees is prohibited at most athletic events, airport terminals, police stations or jails, meetings of government bodies, courthouses, colleges, bars, churches, parades, polling places, places of nuisance and any business or private establishment that posts a sign against carry.

Persons without recognized permits: A license is not required to carry a loaded, concealed handgun anywhere in a vehicle or in a fully enclosed container or holster while on foot. "Enclosed container" would include any closed purse, handbag, satchel or briefcase. "Holster" would include any belt or shoulder holster worn upon the person. The handgun must remain secured in the holster and may not be worn in any other way (ie. tucked into a belt or waistband). Those exercising this "permitless" carry option are still prohibited from carrying in areas off-limits to regular permittees.

Handguns may continue to be carried openly while on foot. If not contained in belt or shoulder holsters, they should remain visible so as not to be "hidden from common observation." Concealment in any manner is lawful if one is involved in target shooting, hunting, or fishing.

All Persons: Standard length long guns may be carried in most public areas and just about anywhere in a vehicle with one important qualification. Hunting laws require long guns in vehicles, or possessed on foot while one is on a public road, to be unloaded during deer & turkey season. The guns may be loaded during other times of the year. This prohibition applies to both permittees and non-permittees.

Businesses may only prohibit firearms inside their buildings. Guns kept in locked vehicles on their parking lots are lawful. And localities may only restrict carry in certain areas such as public parks and meetings. The preemption law sets legal sanctions against cities that attempt overbroad regulation.

Missouri

Total prohibition *(-2, St. Louis enforcing illegal carry ban in public parks)* **Total freedom**

0 ------- 10 ------- 20 ------- 30 ------- 40 ------- 50 ------- 60 ------- 70 ------- 80 ------ 90 ------ 100

^

CHECKLIST

***Standard firearms & ammo:** no permit required for possession or sale – see p. 3
***Semi-auto guns & high capacity magazines:** no permit required for possession or sale
***Machine guns & suppressors:** ownership lawful per federal law compliance
***Firearm law uniformity:** preemption law, gun laws uniform except localities may regulate the open carry of loaded weapons by non-permittees in public areas
***Right of Self-Defense:** NRA-model castle doctrine, *stand your ground* in public areas
***Open carry:** unrestricted under state law; some local regulation of loaded carry is possible
***Licensed concealed carry:** licenses issued on a "shall issue" basis to residents only
***Constitutional or "no permit required" concealed carry:** yes – see below
***Out-of-state permit recognition:** automatic recognition of carry permits from all other states
***Weapons allowed for *licensed* carry:** include any lawful deadly weapon

VEHICLES

***Vehicle carry by non-permittees:** loaded firearms may be carried anywhere in a vehicle
***Vehicle gun possession at colleges:** lawful for permittees, but subject to college policy
***Vehicle gun possession at K-12 schools:** Missouri permittee w/loaded handgun lawful
***Duty to notify LEO of permit/carry status:** upon demand of police officer
***RV carry while "boondocking":** parking lot owners may *not* prohibit guns in vehicles – see p.8

***State Parks:** concealed handgun carry by recognized licensees permitted
***Restaurants serving alcohol:** permittees may carry while eating in dining areas – see p.3
***Hotels:** statutory allowance for guest rejection or ejectment for gun possession – see p.7
***Airports:** carry allowed in non-sterile terminal areas and parking lots – see p.9

Missouri developed a well-earned reputation during the Civil War as a place where personal gun ownership was a necessity for survival. With roving bands of guerillas from both sides exacting a heavy toll on the population, farmers in the hinterland needed plenty of firepower just to stay alive. Missourians continue this tradition today by their recognition of "constitutional carry."

Recognized permittees: Despite allowing concealed carry without a permit (see below), licenses are still issued by local sheriffs to qualified residents who are at least 19 years old, or 18 if a military member, on a "shall issue" basis. These permits are valid for five years and allow the carry of any firearm. Extended term and lifetime licenses are also offered. But these permits are only valid in Missouri and, unlike the 5 year permits, do not qualify for recognition outside Missouri.

Missouri does not issue permits to non-residents but will recognize all other states' carry permits. Recognized permittees may carry openly or concealed in most public areas. But carry is prohibited in law enforcement offices, polling booths, large sports arenas, schools, courthouses, childcare facilities, amusement parks, churches (absent consent of church leadership), government meetings & posted facilities, colleges, hospitals, casinos, bars, and posted private establishments. These restrictions only apply to buildings. Weapons secured in vehicles in parking lots are lawful. And any violation of the above-listed restrictions is not a criminal offense for the permittee who is a first time violator.

Persons without recognized permits: A license is not required to carry a loaded firearm anywhere in a vehicle. The glove compartment, console box or under the seat are all legitimate placement areas. Concealed carry is also allowed on foot as long as such carry does not occur in one of the prohibited areas listed in the preceding paragraph. But unlike permittees, carry by non-permittees in these areas can result in criminal penalties ranging from misdemeanors to, in the case of schools, felony charges. Only a carry violation on posted private property would be a non-criminal offense.

Open carry on foot is allowed in most public areas with one notable exception. Cities may prohibit the open carry of loaded firearms by anyone without a license. Local ordinances exist which prohibit any non-permittee from having an openly displayed, loaded gun in public.

All Persons: Missouri's preemption law prevents most local gun regulation (despite St. Louis' attempts to illegally ban guns in parks). But, be aware, that state law prohibits gun possession by anyone on a bus.

Montana

Total prohibition *(+5, 2020 referendum restricts local power to regulate carry)* **Total freedom**

0 ------- 10 ------- 20 ------- 30 ------- 40 ------- 50 ------- 60 ------- 70 ------- 80 ------ 90 ------ 100

^

CHECKLIST

- ***Standard firearms & ammo:** no permit required for possession or sale – see p.3
- ***Semi-auto guns & high capacity magazines:** no permit required for possession or sale
- ***Machine guns or suppressors:** ownership lawful per federal law compliance
- ***Firearm law uniformity:** preemption law, some local regulation of public buildings possible
- ***Right of Self-Defense:** NRA-model castle doctrine, *stand your ground* in public areas
- ***Open carry:** unrestricted in most public areas and generally accepted
- ***Licensed concealed carry:** licenses issued on a "shall issue" basis to residents only
- ***Constitutional or "no permit required" concealed carry:** limited – see below
- ***Out-of-state permit recognition:** conditional recognition of permits from other states (see p. 65)
- ***Weapons allowed for *licensed* carry:** include handguns, knives and any lawful deadly weapon

VEHICLES

- ***Vehicle carry by non-permittees:** loaded firearms may be carried in plain view, console box, glove compartment or commercial gun case; firearms may not be concealed *on one's person* in a vehicle (see below)
- ***Vehicle gun possession at colleges:** subject to college administrative policy
- ***Vehicle gun possession at K-12 schools:** Montana permittee w/loaded handgun lawful
- ***Duty to notify LEO of permit/carry status:** upon demand of police officer
- ***RV carry while "boondocking":** parking lot owners may restrict gun carry by visitors – see p.8
- ***State Parks:** concealed handgun carry by recognized licensees permitted
- ***Restaurants serving alcohol:** concealed carry prohibited for everyone
- ***Hotels:** prohibited from barring gun possession by guests – see p.7
- ***Airports:** localities may prohibit open carry in all buildings; car carry in parking lots O.K. – see p.9

Montana's vast expanse offers the traveler some breathtaking views as well as ample incentive to carry a firearm for personal protection. The state's historical connections to the "Old West" are vividly reflected in its firearm laws.

Recognized permittees: The state requires a license to carry a concealed weapon within the boundaries of most population centers. The sheriff of an applicant's home county issues permits to qualified residents 18 years or older for four-year terms. Montana does not grant licenses to nonresidents but will recognize the permits of other states under certain conditions. The state that issued the permit must require a background check of applicants prior to permit issuance. And the nonresident permittee must also possess photo identification along with his actual permit if the permit itself has no photo. Recognized permittees can carry concealed in most public areas. Notable exceptions include government buildings, banks & financial institutions, bars, and restaurants serving alcohol.

Persons without recognized permits: Montana allows anyone to carry a concealed firearm when they are outside the boundary of a city, town or logging camp. Persons engaged in outdoor activities such as hiking and camping may also carry concealed firearms without permits.

"Concealed" in Montana is defined as "carrying or bearing concealed upon one's person" a deadly weapon that is "wholly or partially covered by wearing apparel." Absent one of the exceptions noted in the previous paragraph, wearing a handgun under your outer clothing would be illegal. But if the weapon is in plain view or secured from view in such a way as not to be "on your person," the carry of the loaded firearm would be legitimate. In a vehicle, a loaded handgun could be placed in a console box, glove compartment or under one's seat. A long gun could be kept in a gun case or gun rack. Trunk transport would also be acceptable.

Localities may prohibit open or unpermitted concealed carry in publicly owned and occupied buildings. But other areas, including parks and public assemblies, are now off-limits to local control.

All Persons: Open carry is generally accepted and supported by statute. The areas listed as "off-limits" to licensed concealed carry are actually O.K. for open carry. But carry on trains and inside school buildings is prohibited to everyone. And hotels may not prohibit guests from having guns.

Nebraska

Total prohibition *(+0, improved, but still tough for non-permittee travel)* **Total freedom**

0 ------- 10 ------- 20 ------- 30 ------- 40 ------- 50 ------- 60 ------- 70 ------- 80 ------ 90 ------ 100

^

CHECKLIST

- ***Standard firearms & ammo:** no restrictions on possession (handgun sales require permit) see p.3
- ***Semi-auto guns & high capacity magazines:** no permit required for possession or sale
- ***Machine guns & suppressors:** ownership lawful per federal law compliance
- ***Firearm law uniformity:** preemption law, local regulation of concealed carry prohibited
- ***Right of Self-Defense:** no NRA-model castle doctrine, *duty to retreat* in public areas
- ***Open carry:** unrestricted under state law; some local regulation possible
- ***Licensed concealed carry:** licenses issued on a "shall issue" basis to residents only
- ***Constitutional or "no permit required" concealed carry:** no
- ***Out-of-state permit recognition:** conditional recognition of permits from other states (see p.65)
- ***Weapons allowed for *licensed* carry:** limited to handguns only

VEHICLES

- ***Vehicle carry by non-permittees:** shotguns must be unloaded; rifles & handguns may be in plain view and loaded under state law, but local laws may prohibit this; to be safe, all firearms in the passenger compartment should be cased and unloaded
- ***Vehicle gun possession at colleges:** lawful for permittees, but subject to college policy
- ***Vehicle gun possession at K-12 schools:** Nebraska permittee w/loaded handgun lawful
- ***Duty to notify LEO of permit status:** immediately upon official contact (EMS also)
- ***RV carry while "boondocking":** parking lot owners may *not* prohibit *permittees* w/guns – p.8

- ***State Parks:** concealed handgun carry by recognized licensees permitted
- ***Restaurants serving alcohol:** permittees may carry while eating in dining areas – see p.3
- ***Hotels:** subject to hotel policy enforcement & "force of law" posting prohibitions – see p.7
- ***Airports:** carry allowed in non-sterile terminal areas and parking lots – see p.9

Nebraska is in the heart of America's breadbasket and is often a state that travelers pass through on their way to a vacation destination in the Far West. Nebraska will provide recognized permittees with a positive atmosphere for gun carry. But travelers without permits should be aware that, despite preemption of issues affecting permit holders, Nebraska still allows localities to regulate firearms carry by non-licensees.

Recognized permittees: A license is required to carry a concealed handgun in a vehicle or on or about one's person. Permits are issued by the State Patrol to qualified residents who are at least 21 years old. They are valid for 5 years, cost $100.00 and allow handgun carry only. Nebraska recognizes out-of-state licenses from states that have equal or greater issuance standards. Recognized permittees may not be residents of Nebraska and must be at least 21 years old. When approached by police or EMS, a permittee must declare that he is carrying a concealed handgun. Places off-limits to carry include banks, bars, churches, schools, athletic events, colleges, hospitals, political rallies, polling booths, government meetings, courthouses, police stations & jails and any posted private property or business. Parking lot possession is lawful if the gun stays locked in the vehicle's glove compartment or trunk or, in the case of a motorcycle, the hardened compartment securely attached to the bike.

Persons without recognized permits: Concealed carry of a loaded handgun is prohibited either in a vehicle or while a person is on foot. Loaded handguns in a vehicle should be stowed in the trunk. A handgun that is *unloaded* may be kept in a closed commercial gun case inside the vehicle. But loaded handguns that are hidden from view and readily accessible (ie. under the seat or in an unlocked glove compartment) are illegal. While on foot, the handgun must be in a visible belt holster and not be in violation of a local ordinance prohibiting open carry. Affirmative defenses to a charge of carrying concealed exist. A traveler who can prove the necessity of carry for self-defense may successfully defend against a conviction.

All Persons: Loaded rifles in a vehicle must be in plain view or cased and kept in the passenger compartment or trunk. Shotguns transported in a vehicle must be unloaded and may be in plain view or enclosed in gun cases. Nebraska's concealed carry law only applies to handgun carry. Permittees and non-permittees must observe the same rules for long gun transport.

Nevada

Total prohibition *(+0, it's pro-gun status is tarnished by political "purpling")* **Total freedom**

0 ------- 10 ------- 20 ------- 30 ------- 40 ------- 50 ------- 60 ------- 70 ------- 80 ------ 90 ------ 100

^ (approximately 90)

CHECKLIST

***Standard firearms & ammo:** no permit required for possession or sale - see p. 3
***Semi-auto guns & high capacity magazines:** no permit required for possession or sale
***Machine guns & suppressors:** ownership lawful per federal law compliance; bump stocks prohibited
***Firearm law uniformity:** preemption law; laws uniform throughout state, all local ordinances, including those in Clark County, are eliminated; localities may be sued for violations
***Right of Self-Defense:** NRA-model castle doctrine, *stand your ground* in public areas
***Open carry:** unrestricted under state law and commonly accepted
***Licensed concealed carry:** licenses issued on a "shall issue" basis to residents and nonresidents
***Constitutional or "no permit required" concealed carry:** no
***Out-of-state permit recognition:** conditional recognition of permits from other states (see p. 65)
***Weapons allowed for *licensed* carry:** limited to handguns only

VEHICLES

***Vehicle carry by non-permittees:** rifles and shotguns carried in a vehicle must be "unloaded;" loaded handguns may be carried openly or in the glove compartment or console box but may not be concealed upon one's person
***Vehicle gun possession at colleges:** prohibited absent written permission from authorities
***Vehicle gun possession at K-12 schools:** prohibited absent written permission from authorities
***Duty to notify LEO of permit status:** upon demand of police officer
***RV carry while "boondocking":** parking lot owners may restrict gun carry by visitors – see p.8

***State Parks:** concealed handgun carry by recognized licensees permitted
***Restaurants serving alcohol:** permittees may carry while eating in dining areas – see p.3
***Hotels:** subject to hotel policy enforcement – see p.7
***Airports:** carry in passenger terminals prohibited; car carry in parking lots O.K. – see p.9

Nevada's open country formerly provided a political atmosphere that was patently gun-friendly. But with the recent passage of "bump stock" bans and child storage laws, demographic shifts may be signaling an ominous move in the wrong direction for gun owners in the Silver State.

Recognized permittees: Licenses to carry concealed handguns are issued to residents and nonresidents who are at least 21 years old or, if members of the armed forces, 18-20 years old. A resident must apply to his local sheriff while a nonresident may apply to any county sheriff. Licenses are valid for five years and apply to handguns only. Permits of nonresidents from states with similar laws are also recognized. Permittees may carry anywhere in the state except K-12 schools, child care facilities, universities, "secure" facilities, public airports and posted public buildings with security screenings or signage prohibiting firearms.

Persons without recognized permits: A traveler may possess a loaded handgun in a vehicle if the weapon is in plain view or secured in the glove compartment or console box. A handgun may not be concealed "upon one's person." A weapon hidden under one's clothing or in a container carried by the person would be illegal. But a loaded handgun secured in a gun case on an empty passenger seat would be O.K.

On foot, a non-permittee may carry a handgun as long as the weapon is visible (ie. snapped belt holster). This carry mode is common in rural areas but unlikely to be seen in Las Vegas.

All Persons: Vehicle carry of rifles and shotguns is allowed as long as the firearms are unloaded and not concealed on one's person. "Unloaded" in Nevada is defined as a firearm that has no live cartridge in the firing chamber. Magazines for rifles and shotguns may remain loaded. This restriction applies to both permittees and non-permittees.

Nevada's preemption law prohibits localities from enacting or enforcing laws regulating transportation, carrying, ownership, sale, and possession of firearms. Recently, the state strengthened its preemption statute to eliminate all local ordinances regulating guns except those prohibiting discharge within local limits. Even resident handgun registration in Clark County is null and void. Localities that attempt enforcement of any local carry law could face civil liablity.

New Hampshire

Total prohibition ***(+0, permitless carry w/ no apology, who says Yankees don't like guns!)*** **Total freedom**

0 ------- 10 ------- 20 ------- 30 ------- 40 ------- 50 ------- 60 ------- 70 ------- 80 ------ 90 ------ 100

^

CHECKLIST

***Standard firearms & ammo:** no permit required for possession or sale – see p.3
***Semi-auto guns & high capacity magazines:** no permit required for possession or sale
***Machine guns & suppressors:** ownership lawful per federal law compliance
***Firearm law uniformity:** preemption law; firearm laws uniform throughout the state
***Right of Self-Defense:** NRA-model castle doctrine, *stand your ground* in public areas
***Open carry:** unrestricted under state law and generally accepted
***Licensed concealed carry:** licenses issued on a "shall issue" basis to residents and nonresidents
***Constitutional or "no permit required" concealed carry:** yes – see below
***Out-of-state permit recognition:** conditional recognition of permits from other states (see p. 65)
***Weapons allowed for *licensed* carry:** limited to handguns only

VEHICLES

***Vehicle carry by non-permittees:** handguns may be loaded and carried concealed or openly anywhere in a motor vehicle; rifles and shotguns must remain unloaded
***Vehicle gun possession at colleges:** subject to college administrative policy
***Vehicle gun possession at K-12 schools:** New Hampshire permittee w/loaded handgun lawful
***Duty to notify LEO of permit/carry status:** upon demand of police officer
***RV carry while "boondocking":** parking lot owners may restrict gun carry by visitors – see p.8

***State Parks:** concealed handgun carry by licensees and those exercising constitutional carry permitted
***Restaurants serving alcohol:** permittees may carry while eating in dining areas – see p.3
***Hotels:** subject to hotel policy enforcement – see p.7
***Airports:** carry allowed in non-sterile terminal areas and parking lots – see p.9

Citizens of New Hampshire are proud of their state's dedication to personal liberties. New Hampshire's motto, "Live Free or Die," was vividly illustrated when the state legislature enacted "constitutional" concealed carry in 2017. The state's geographical location in the restrictive northeast does not prevent the "Granite State" from being one of America's best.

Recognized permittees: Despite no longer being required, New Hampshire still issues licenses to carry loaded handguns in a vehicle or concealed upon one's person through the police chief or sheriff of a resident's hometown for 5-year terms. Permits are also issued to nonresidents through the state police. Nonresident permits cost $100.00 and no longer require the applicant to have a carry permit from his home state. Such licenses provide a distinct advantage when traveling to states that still require a license to carry a handgun; thus providing ample incentive for application and issuance. The New Hampshire State police continue to execute reciprocity arrangements with qualifying states.

Persons without recognized permits: Anyone who is not otherwise prohibited from possessing a firearm (felon, minor, etc.) may carry a loaded handgun in a vehicle. The weapon may be displayed openly or kept concealed on the person. Stowage in a gun case, glove compartment or console box is also acceptable.

Carry of a loaded handgun (openly or concealed) while on foot is similarly allowed in most public areas except those mentioned in the "all persons" section below. New Hampshire's preemption law prevents localities from regulating this and most other aspects of gun ownership.

All Persons: Rifles and shotguns in a vehicle must be unloaded and should be kept in gun cases, gun racks, or trunks. Magazines for these weapons may remain loaded as long as they are not attached to any firearm. Current statutes still prohibit *loaded* long gun transport in vehicles for everyone. So even recognized licensees must keep their rifles and shotguns unloaded while traveling.

Carry is allowed in most public areas except courthouses and posted property. Even K-12 school facilities are not prohibited if one possesses a New Hampshire permit and is not a student at the school. A recent A.G. opinion found that local schools lack the power to impose their own gun bans as well.

New Jersey

Total prohibition *(+0, a good example of how bad things can truly become)* **Total freedom**

0 ------- 10 ------- 20 ------- 30 ------- 40 ------- 50 ------- 60 ------- 70 ------- 80 ------ 90 ------ 100

^

CHECKLIST

***Standard firearms & ammo:** restricted, carry permit needed for handgun possession unless exception applies; firearm purchaser identification card required for long guns; hollow point ammo prohibited unless kept at home

***Semi-auto guns & high capacity magazines:** restricted, all "assault weapons" and any over 10 shot magazines are banned from entering the state; bump stocks prohibited

***Machine guns & suppressors:** personal ownership prohibited

***Firearm law uniformity:** firearm laws are strict, no state preemption

***Right of Self-Defense:** no NRA-model castle doctrine, *duty to retreat* in public areas

***Open carry:** prohibited in all public areas unless one has a New Jersey carry permit

***Licensed concealed carry:** licenses issued on a "may issue" basis to residents and nonresidents

***Constitutional or "no permit required" concealed carry:** no

***Out-of-state permit recognition:** no recognition of out-of-state carry permits

***Weapons allowed for *licensed* carry:** limited to handguns only

VEHICLES

***Vehicle carry by non-permittees:** firearms may not be carried in a vehicle without a purchaser identification card or NJ carry permit (exception for interstate transport – see p.5)

***Vehicle gun possession at colleges:** prohibited by law

***Vehicle gun possession at K-12 schools:** firearm possession prohibited

***Duty to notify LEO of permit status:** upon demand of police officer

***RV carry while "boondocking":** parking lot owners may restrict gun carry by visitors – see p.8

***State Parks:** firearms possession or use prohibited

***Restaurants serving alcohol:** permittees may carry while eating in dining areas – see p.3

***Hotels:** subject to hotel policy enforcement – see p.7

***Airports:** carry allowed in non-sterile terminal areas and parking lots (watch for local postings)

Travelers to New Jersey should be prepared for highly restrictive firearm laws. The state's urban demographics and left-wing political bent have made it a hell house for gun owners.

New Jersey permittees: New Jersey requires a license to carry a loaded handgun on your person or in a vehicle. New Jersey residents may apply to their local police chief for such a permit. Non-residents must apply directly to the Superintendent of State Police. Such licenses are then issued by a state Superior court for a two-year term and are granted on a highly discretionary basis. The state does not recognize any out-of-state permits. And thanks to efforts by Gov. Phil Murphy, permit issuance standards remain strict. Citizens will find it impossible to obtain a permit absent a "compelling" need.

Persons without New Jersey permits: Handgun possession outside of one's home or business generally requires a carry permit issued by a New Jersey Superior court. Rifle and shotgun possession requires a firearm purchaser identification card issued by a person's local police chief or by the state police if the applicant is an out-of-state resident. An ID card or permit is also required for vehicle transport of these firearms. Strict exceptions to this prohibition allow the transport of unloaded and securely cased firearms without a card or permit if a person is traveling directly to a hunting engagement, firearms exhibition, repair facility or target range. But general transport within the state is prohibited. Travelers w/o an ID card or failing to qualify for an exception should leave all firearms at home unless transporting per McClure-Volkmer (p.5).

Open carry of a handgun without a New Jersey license is strictly prohibited. New Jersey does not differentiate between open or concealed carry. Both carry modes are prohibited unless one is engaged in hunting or shooting activity in an area officially sanctioned for such pursuit.

All Persons: Personal ownership of military-pattern semi-automatic weapons, bump stocks, over 10 shot magazines, machine guns and most hollow point handgun ammo is prohibited. Travelers should take care to leave all such items behind when traveling to New Jersey. An exception exists for residents to keep hollow point ammunition in their homes and to permanently block any magazines over 10 shots. But importation of such items by nonresident travelers is prohibited.

New Mexico

Total prohibition *(-5, Albuquerque enforcing illegal carry bans in city limits)* **Total freedom**

0 ------- 10 ------- 20 ------- 30 ------- 40 ------- 50 ------- 60 ------- 70 ------- 80 ------ 90 ------ 100

^

CHECKLIST

- ***Standard firearms & ammo:** no permit required for possession or sale – see p.3
- ***Semi-auto guns & high capacity magazines:** no permit required for possession or sale
- ***Machine guns & suppressors:** ownership lawful per federal law compliance
- ***Firearm law uniformity:** preemption law, firearm laws uniform throughout state
- ***Right of Self-Defense:** no NRA castle doctrine, *stand your ground* in public not codified
- ***Open carry:** unrestricted in most public areas and generally accepted
- ***Licensed concealed carry:** licenses issued on a "shall issue" basis to residents only
- ***Constitutional or "no permit required" concealed carry:** no
- ***Out-of-state permit recognition:** conditional recognition of permits from other states (see p. 65)
- ***Weapons allowed for *licensed* carry:** limited to only one handgun at a time

VEHICLES

- ***Vehicle carry by non-permittees:** loaded, concealed firearms may be carried anywhere in a private automobile for self-protection
- ***Vehicle gun possession at colleges:** lawful for anyone over 19, subject to college policy
- ***Vehicle gun possession at K-12 schools:** New Mexico permittee w/loaded handgun lawful
- ***Duty to notify LEO of permit status:** upon demand of police officer
- ***RV carry while "boondocking":** parking lot owners may restrict gun carry by visitors – see p.8

- ***State Parks:** concealed handgun carry by recognized licensees permitted
- ***Restaurants serving alcohol:** permittees allowed to carry with qualification (see below)
- ***Hotels:** subject to hotel policy enforcement & "force of law" posting prohibitions – see p.7
- ***Airports:** carry allowed in non-sterile terminal areas and parking lots – see p.9

New Mexico was named the "Land of Enchantment" for its rugged mountain terrain and vast prairie tracts. Gun ownership has always been an important part of life for New Mexicans. As late as 1916, citizens in the southern border town of Columbus used their privately owned arms to help Army units repel an attack by Mexican bandit Pancho Villa. This incident illustrates the well-established historical imperative for gun ownership in this frontier state of the Southwest.

Recognized permittees: New Mexico requires a license to carry a loaded, concealed handgun while on foot. Licenses are issued to residents on a "shall issue" basis through the Department of Public Safety and are granted for four-year terms to persons 21 years or older. New Mexico will not issue permits to nonresidents but will recognize permits from other states that have reciprocity agreements with New Mexico. A recognized permittee is limited to carrying only one handgun at a time. He must also be a U.S. citizen and at least 21 years old. Carry is prohibited on any "posted" property as well as on tribal lands, colleges and courthouses. Permittees can carry in restaurants that serve beer and wine but not ones that serve hard liquor.

Persons without recognized permits: Vehicle carry of firearms is unrestricted. Loaded, concealed firearms may be carried in the passenger compartment or trunk. Under the seat, in the glove compartment or concealed in a purse are all legitimate placement areas.

A non-permittee on foot can similarly carry an *unloaded* firearm anywhere on his person. The weapon may be concealed from view in a snapped belt holster or secured in a commercial gun case. Loaded handguns may be openly carried on foot in most public places. One area off-limits to such carry and, of most importance to the traveler, is any retail establishment that sells, distributes or serves alcohol. Loaded or unloaded carry in these areas is punishable as a felony unless one has a recognized permit or fits into a statutory exception.

All Persons: Open or concealed carry is prohibited to all persons on public buses, game preserves, university campuses, K-12 schools, courthouses and restaurants that serve hard liquor. The state's preemption law prohibits most local ordinances that could create even more restricted areas. But Albuquerque is enforcing carry prohibitions in areas such as parks and government buildings despite state preemption. Travelers should look for postings until the courts strike down these bans. And 18 year olds from other states should be aware that handgun possession is limited to persons 19 years and older.

New York

Total prohibition *(+0, Bloomberg, DeBlasio & Cuomo; can it get any worse?)* **Total freedom**

0 ------- 10 ------- 20 ------- 30 ------- 40 ------- 50 ------- 60 ------- 70 ------- 80 ------ 90 ------ 100

^ (20)

CHECKLIST

***Standard firearms & ammo:** restricted, permit required for handgun possession; no license required for long gun possession; ammo sales restricted, but possession is not

***Semi-auto guns & high capacity magazines:** restricted; "assault weapons" and magazines over 10 shots may not be imported; bump stocks prohibited

***Machine guns & suppressors:** personal ownership prohibited

***Firearm law uniformity:** some local regulation, especially in New York City

***Right of Self-Defense:** no NRA-model castle doctrine, *duty to retreat* in public areas

***Open carry:** prohibited in all public areas

***Licensed concealed carry:** licenses issued on "may issue" basis to residents & some nonresidents

***Constitutional or "no permit required" concealed carry:** no

***Out-of-state permit recognition:** no recognition of out-of-state carry permits

***Weapons allowed for *licensed* carry:** limited to handguns only

VEHICLES

***Vehicle carry for non-permittees:** rifles and shotguns must be unloaded; handgun possession or carry requires a New York license

***Vehicle gun possession at colleges:** prohibited by law

***Vehicle gun possession at K-12 schools:** firearm possession prohibited

***Duty to notify LEO of permit status:** upon demand of police officer

***RV carry while "boondocking":** parking lot owners may restrict gun carry by visitors – see p.8

***State Parks:** firearm possession or use prohibited; limited exceptions for "special permit" hunting

***Restaurants serving alcohol:** permittees may carry while eating in dining areas – see p.3

***Hotels:** subject to hotel policy enforcement – see p.7

***Airports:** some airports, such as Syracuse, ban carry on all property – watch for local postings

New York is typical of many eastern seaboard states in that licensing and registration of firearms have been well established for decades. Since 1911, mere possession of a handgun by a New York resident, even in one's own home, requires a New York license to possess or carry.

New York permittees: New York requires a license to possess or carry a handgun. Such permits are issued to residents on a discretionary basis through their home county. If the license has no stated restrictions, the permittee may carry the handgun loaded and concealed. Open carry is not allowed for anyone, including licensees. New York does not issue licenses to nonresidents unless the person is *principally employed* within the state (ie. bank guards) or lives in New York part-time. And New York will not honor out-of-state permits. This makes handgun carry by the out-of-state traveler, either in a vehicle or on one's person, nearly impossible.

Persons without New York permits: A traveler may transport his handgun through the state if the weapon is unloaded and secured in a locked case in the trunk or storage area. The traveler's ultimate destination must also be a state where unlicensed possession is permitted. Any extended stops in New York would render the "through" nature of the trip void and thus subject the traveler to prosecution by state authorities. A traveler should carry proof of hotel reservations in his destination state to prove the interstate nature of his trip.

All Persons: Anyone may transport standard rifles and shotguns into New York without a license as long as the weapons are unloaded (ammunition is in separate boxes) and secured in commercial gun cases. This would apply even if one possesses a New York pistol permit. Machine guns, semi-automatic *assault weapons* and over 10 shot magazines are prohibited from importation. A federal judge struck down a mandate that limited loaded magazines to no more than (7) rounds. But the case is still being litigated. So gun owners should keep abreast of changes. New York is strict enough to define a "loaded" handgun as being one in which ammo for the weapon is simply in close proximity. So beware!

The possession of any firearm in the City of New York without a New York City license is strictly prohibited. But persons transporting standard rifles and shotguns through the City may do so for a 24-hr. period after entering the City if the weapons are unloaded and locked in cases.

North Carolina

Total prohibition *(+0, election maps make it purple, but for guns, it's solid red!)* **Total freedom**

0 ------- 10 ------- 20 ------- 30 ------- 40 ------- 50 ------- 60 ------- 70 ------- 80 ------ 90 ------ 100

^

CHECKLIST

***Standard firearms & ammo:** no restrictions on possession; handgun sales require permit
***Semi-auto guns & high capacity magazines:** no permit required for possession or sale
***Machine guns & suppressors:** permit from sheriff for machine guns, otherwise federal law applies
***Firearm law uniformity:** preemption law, but some carry restrictions at the local level possible
***Right of Self-Defense:** NRA-model castle doctrine, *stand your ground* in public areas
***Open carry:** unrestricted under state law except for certain specified public areas
***Licensed concealed carry:** licenses issued on a "shall issue" basis to residents only
***Constitutional or "no permit required" concealed carry:** no
***Out-of-state permit recognition:** automatic recognition of carry permits from all other states
***Weapons allowed for *licensed* carry:** limited to handguns only

VEHICLES

***Vehicle carry by non-permittees:** loaded firearms may be secured in holsters or slings and carried openly in the passenger compartment (concealed guns should be in trunk)
***Vehicle gun possession at colleges:** lawful for permittees, private schools may prohibit
***Vehicle gun possession at K-12 schools:** North Carolina permittee w/loaded handgun lawful (but *private* schools may still prohibit all firearms possession)
***Duty to notify LEO of permit status:** immediately upon official contact
***RV carry while "boondocking":** parking lot owners may restrict gun carry by visitors – see p.8

***State Parks:** concealed handgun carry by recognized licensees permitted
***Restaurants serving alcohol:** permittees may carry if premises are not "posted" – see p.3
***Hotels:** subject to hotel policy enforcement & "force of law" posting prohibitions – see p.7
***Airports:** localities may prohibit carry in terminal areas; car carry in parking lots O.K. – see p.9

The beautiful scenery of the Blue Ridge Mountains as well as the state's user-friendly firearm laws will impress visitors to North Carolina. The state's rural areas, in particular, provide a vivid reminder that Andy Griffith's Mayberry is alive and well in the Tar Heel state.

Recognized permittees: North Carolina issues licenses to carry concealed, loaded handguns to qualified residents 21 years or older for 5 year terms. North Carolina does not issue permits to nonresidents but will recognize permits from all other states. When approached by police, a permittee must declare that he has a handgun with a valid permit. Permittees may carry in most public areas except state government offices, the state capitol, courthouses, educational properties (including colleges), the state fair & posted prohibited areas. Handguns in closed compartments within locked vehicles parked on government & state educational premises, courthouses and the state fair are lawful.

Persons without recognized permits: Vehicle carry of loaded handguns is limited to those weapons that are in plain view. A pistol placed in a hip holster or on the vehicle's dash or passenger seat is acceptable if the weapon remains visible from outside the vehicle. But courts have held that any concealment of a readily accessible handgun could constitute carrying a concealed weapon. And because concealment includes any gun "on or about the person," stowage in a glove compartment or console box is not advisable. Instead, handguns that are hidden from view should be in the trunk or rear-most portion of the vehicle and secured in gun cases.

Open carry of a loaded handgun while on foot is lawful in many public areas. But carry by non-permittees is still prohibited at funeral processions, parades, educational properties (including universities & colleges), places where alcohol is served, the state capitol and North Carolina courts.

All Persons: Loaded long guns may be kept in racks or slings if they remain visible. Or they may be cased in the trunk or rear-most cargo area as long as they are not concealed about one's person.

Both permittees and non-permittees are prohibited from carrying guns at public demonstrations and picket lines. And while localities may ban carry in parks, recreational centers and publicly owned buildings such as airports by posting signs, vehicle possession in these areas is O.K. for everyone.

No all-inclusive parking lot storage law exits in North Carolina. So some property owners may still prohibit guns in all areas, including vehicles parked on their lots.

North Dakota

Total prohibition *(+0, good for residents & permittees, nonresidents w/o permits – ouch!)* **Total freedom**

0 ------- 10 ------- 20 ------- 30 ------- 40 ------- 50 ------- 60 ------- 70 ------- 80 ------ 90 ------ 100

^

CHECKLIST

- ***Standard firearms & ammo:** no permit required for possession or sale – see p. 3
- ***Semi-auto guns & high capacity magazines:** no permit required for possession or sale
- ***Machine guns & suppressors:** ownership lawful per federal law compliance
- ***Firearm law uniformity:** preemption law, local regulation of some carry *not* preempted
- ***Right of Self-Defense:** NRA-model castle doctrine, *stand your ground* in vehicle only
- ***Open carry:** loaded carry prohibited for non-permittees – (some exceptions - see below)
- ***Licensed concealed carry:** licenses issued on a "shall issue" basis to residents and nonresidents
- ***Constitutional or "no permit required" concealed carry:** limited – see below
- ***Out-of-state permit recognition:** conditional recognition of permits from other states (see p. 65)
- ***Weapons allowed for licensed carry:** include any lawful deadly weapon

VEHICLES

- ***Vehicle carry by non-permittees:** non residents must have all firearms unloaded and secured in gun cases or closed trunks; qualified residents may possess concealed, loaded firearms
- ***Vehicle gun possession at colleges:** lawful for anyone (permittees or non-permittees)
- ***Vehicle gun possession at K-12 schools:** North Dakota permittee w/loaded handgun lawful under state law, but some localities may enforce their own prohibitive policies
- ***Duty to notify LEO of permit/carry status:** upon demand for permittees only (see below)
- ***RV carry while "boondocking":** parking lot owners may *not* prohibit guns in vehicles – see p.8

- ***State Parks:** concealed handgun carry by recognized licensees permitted
- ***Restaurants serving alcohol:** permittees may carry if area is open to those under 21 – see p.3
- ***Hotels:** subject to hotel policy enforcement; statutory exception for loaded gun in room – see p.7
- ***Airports:** carry prohibited in most passenger terminals; car carry in parking lots O.K. – see p.9

North Dakota's frigid winters can make one of America's northern-most states appear pretty uninviting. But the harsh climate has helped to forge a population of hardy souls that call upon firearms for daily use more often than most. Teddy Roosevelt even used his considerable skill as a rifleman to apprehend frontier ruffians who stole a boat from his ranch. Occurrences like this exemplify the gun culture that led to the recent passage of a "residents only" constitutional carry law.

Recognized permittees: Licenses to carry loaded guns in a vehicle or concealed on one's person are still issued through the Bureau of Criminal Investigation to qualified persons 18 years & older for 5 year terms. They are divided into Class I and Class II permits and allow the open or concealed carry of any firearm. North Dakota grants permits to nonresidents and will recognize any permit issued by a state that also recognizes North Dakota.

Persons without recognized permits: Nonresidents without recognized permits (or residents not qualifying for permitless carry) must keep firearms in a vehicle unloaded and secured in commercial gun cases or the trunk. To be unloaded, a firearm's chamber must be empty. Revolvers must also have all chambers in the cylinder empty. Magazines for any firearm may contain ammunition.

A person who has been a resident for at least one year and is otherwise qualified for a Class 2 license (at least 18 yrs old) may carry a concealed, loaded firearm without a permit while on foot or in a vehicle. He must possess a photo ID that verifies his ND residency, keep the gun concealed and immediately inform a policeman upon official contact that he has a firearm. Unlike permittees, the duty to inform for those exercising permitless carry is "upon official contact."

Non-residents without permits may carry loaded handguns on foot while engaged in hunting and target shooting. And loaded carry at a temporary residence (ie. campsite, hotel room) is also permissible. But any other loaded carry by nonresidents (such as open carry) would require a recognized license.

All Persons: Everyone, including recognized permittees, is forbidden from carrying firearms in bars, casinos, gaming sites and "public gatherings." "Public gatherings" would include athletic events, schools, churches (absent written permission from church), and public buildings (excluding rest areas & restrooms). Firearms kept within vehicles are lawful at these locations, universities and most work sites.

Ohio

Total prohibition *(+0, solid work at the grass roots makes the buckeye state shine!)* **Total freedom**

0 ------- 10 ------- 20 ------- 30 ------ 40 ------- 50 ------ 60 ------- 70 ------- 80 ------- 90 ------ 100

^

CHECKLIST

***Standard firearms & ammo:** no permit required for possession or sale – see p.3
***Semi-auto guns & high capacity magazines:** no permit required for possession or sale
***Machine guns & suppressors:** safe storage required & federal law compliance
***Firearm law uniformity:** preemption law, firearm laws uniform throughout state
***Right of Self-Defense:** NRA-model castle doctrine, *stand your ground* in vehicle only
***Open carry:** unrestricted under state law and becoming more accepted
***Licensed concealed carry:** licenses issued on a "shall issue" basis to residents and nonresidents
***Constitutional or "no permit required" concealed carry:** no
***Out-of-state permit recognition:** automatic recognition of all nonresidents with carry permits
***Weapons allowed for *licensed* carry:** limited to handguns only

VEHICLES

***Vehicle carry by non-permittees:** firearms must be unloaded, the weapons must be in plain view with actions open or enclosed in cases
***Vehicle gun possession at colleges:** lawful for permittees, but preempted policies may exist
***Vehicle gun possession at K-12 schools:** Ohio permittee w/loaded handgun lawful
***Duty to notify LEO of permit/carry status:** immediately upon official contact
***RV carry while "boondocking":** parking lot owners may *not* prohibit permittees w/guns – p.8

***State Parks:** concealed handgun carry by recognized licensees in outdoor areas permitted
***Restaurants serving alcohol:** permittees may carry while eating in dining areas – see p. 3
***Hotels:** subject to hotel policy enforcement & "force of law" posting prohibitions – see p.7
***Airports:** carry allowed in non-sterile terminal areas and parking lots unless posted – see p.9

Ohio has made great improvements in its gun laws recently. These advancements are worth noting because the state is often considered a bellwether for national trends.

Recognized permittees / persons: A license is required to carry a concealed, loaded handgun. The sheriff of a person's home county or an adjacent county will issue a license to any qualified person 21 years or older for a five-year term. Ohio will issue licenses to nonresidents who are employed in Ohio and will recognize the out-of-state permit of any nonresident. Residents with permits from states that have reciprocity agreements with Ohio are also recognized. And active duty military members with valid military IDs & proof of required training may carry as if they were permittees.

During a traffic stop, a recognized licensee or qualified military member must remain in his vehicle, keep his hands in plain sight and may not touch or attempt to grasp the handgun. He must also immediately inform the officer that he has a carry license or a military ID with a handgun.

A permittee / qualified military member may not carry in police stations or jails, colleges (unless authorized), bars (unless permittee is *not* consuming alcohol), churches (unless church grants permission), mental health centers, courthouses, government buildings where official business is conducted and any posted private businesses. But most state & local government buildings that are primarily used as restroom or rest area facilities are O.K. for carry. And parking lots of these areas are lawful if the handgun stays in the car and is kept in a locked compartment when the car is unoccupied.

Persons without recognized permits: Vehicle transport is limited to an unloaded firearm that is in plain view with actions open or secured in a closed commercial gun case, gun rack or trunk.

A non-permittee may openly carry a loaded handgun while on foot in most unrestricted public areas. Such carry is legitimate under state statutes and protected from local regulation by Ohio's preemption law.

All Persons: Rifles and shotguns in a vehicle must be unloaded and secured in gun cases regardless of one's permit status. Permittees have no special carry privileges with long guns.

Non-permittees, and permittees transporting long guns, may carry loaded magazines in the trunk or any container that provides "separate enclosure" for the items. Magazine & gun may be in the same container as long as the magazine is in a separate compartment within that container.

Oklahoma

Total prohibition *(+0, Oil, cattle & guns – 3 staples that Okies can't do without)* **Total freedom**

0 ------- 10 ------- 20 ------- 30 ------- 40 ------- 50 ------- 60 ------- 70 ------- 80 ------ 90 ------ 100

^

CHECKLIST

***Standard firearms & ammo:** no restrictions, except carry limited to ammo that is .45 or less
***Semi-auto guns & high capacity magazines:** no permit required for possession or sale
***Machine guns & suppressors:** ownership lawful per federal law compliance
***Firearm law uniformity:** preemption law, firearm laws uniform throughout state
***Right of Self-Defense:** NRA-model castle doctrine, *stand your ground* in public areas
***Open carry:** unrestricted under state law per recent passage of "constitutional carry"
***Licensed concealed carry:** licenses issued on a "shall issue" basis to residents only
***Constitutional or "no permit required" concealed carry:** yes – see below
***Out-of-state permit recognition:** automatic recognition of carry permits from all other states
***Weapons allowed for *licensed* carry:** carry limited to handguns .45 or less

VEHICLES

***Vehicle carry by non-permittees:** loaded handguns may be carried anywhere in a vehicle; long guns must be chamber-unloaded but may be kept in passenger compartment or trunk
***Vehicle gun possession at colleges:** lawful for any gun owner
***Vehicle gun possession at K-12 schools:** Oklahoma permittee w/loaded handgun lawful
***Duty to notify LEO of permit/carry status:** upon demand of police officer
***RV carry while "boondocking":** parking lot owners may *not* prohibit guns in vehicles – see p.8

***State Parks:** recognized licensees may carry in open areas, but not in any gov't buildings
***Restaurants serving alcohol:** permittees may carry while eating in dining areas – see p.3
***Hotels:** subject to hotel policy enforcement – see p.7
***Airports:** carry prohibited in any government-owned terminal; carry in parking lots O.K. – see p. 9

Oklahoma was opened to pioneer settlement after most of the West had already been "won." This frontier connection is perhaps what inspired the Sooner State to enact "constitutional carry" in 2019. Despite an already friendly atmosphere for gun ownership, the carry options this new law provides for the average citizen make the landscape for Okies and their visitors all the better.

Recognized permittees: Oklahoma still issues licenses to carry loaded handguns on foot or in a vehicle to residents who are 21 years or older (or 18-20 years old if member of armed forces) for 5 or 10 year terms. The state will recognize all out-of-state carry permits as well as any military ID issued to a member of the armed forces. Recognized permittees may carry *holstered* handguns (.45 or less) openly or concealed in most public areas except those places listed in the "all persons" section below.

Persons without recognized permits: Any law-abiding person 21 or older (or 18-20 if member or veteran of the armed forces) may carry a loaded firearm (handgun, rifle or shotgun) openly or concealed without a permit in most public areas (see "all persons'). Firearms may also be carried anywhere in a vehicle. But while handguns may be loaded in the magazine & chamber, rifles and shotguns must remain chamber-unloaded.

Those exercising the "no permit required" option may not have prior violations involving illegal drug use, domestic abuse, stalking or aggravated assault. And some places, such as restaurants serving alcohol, remain off-limits unless one possesses a carry license.

All Persons: Carry is prohibited to everyone in bars, sports arenas, casinos, K-12 schools, colleges & universities, technology centers, most government-owned buildings (including those at rest areas, state parks and airports), and posted private businesses. Vehicle gun possession in parking lots for these areas is lawful. Wildlife refuges, parks, fairgrounds and recreational areas are O.K. for carry as long the carry does not occur within any building or office space located on the site. And carry of a *concealed* handgun is allowed on some municipal zoo & park property.

Oklahoma prevents property owners from enforcing policies that restrict the carry of firearms and ammunition in vehicles parked on their lots. And entry into posted private businesses carries no criminal penalty unless one refuses to leave. Oklahoma's preemption law prevents most local regulation of carry rights and even allows civil suits against localities that violate its provisions.

Oregon

Total prohibition *(+0, no reciprocity & limited preemption keep rating below 80)* **Total freedom**

0 ------- 10 ------- 20 ------- 30 ------- 40 ------- 50 ------- 60 ------- 70 ------- 80 ------ 90 ------ 100

^

CHECKLIST

***Standard firearms & ammo:** no permit required for possession or sale – see p. 3

***Semi-auto guns & high capacity magazines:** no permit required for possession or sale

***Machine guns & suppressors:** ownership lawful per federal law compliance

***Firearm law uniformity:** preemption statute, but local regulation of loaded gun carry possible

***Right of Self-Defense:** no NRA castle doctrine, *stand your ground* in public not codified

***Open carry:** unrestricted under state law; some local regulation may exist

***Licensed concealed carry:** licenses issued on a "shall issue" basis to residents; nonresidents from contiguous states must demonstrate a "compelling business interest" or legitimate need

***Constitutional or "no permit required" concealed carry:** no

***Out-of-state permit recognition:** no recognition of out-of-state carry permits

***Weapons allowed for *licensed* carry:** limited to handguns only

VEHICLES

***Vehicle carry by non-permittees:** loaded firearms must be carried in plain view or securely encased in the trunk or storage compartment (local restrictions possible) – see below

***Vehicle gun possession at colleges:** lawful for Oregon permittees only

***Vehicle gun possession at K-12 schools:** Oregon permittee w/loaded handgun lawful

***Duty to notify LEO of permit status:** upon demand of police officer

***RV carry while "boondocking":** lot owners may restrict, but law protects carry otherwise - p.8

***State Parks:** Oregon permittees may carry concealed handguns

***Restaurants serving alcohol:** permittees may carry while eating in dining areas – see p.3

***Hotels:** subject to hotel policy enforcement – see p.7

***Airports:** carry allowed for Oregon permittes in non-sterile terminal areas and parking lots – see p.9

Oregon's proximity to the highly regulated state of California might cause some to expect gun laws that mirror those of its southern neighbor. While gun carry options for nonresidents could be better, most travelers will find Oregon's timber-rich countryside to be gun-friendly.

Oregon permittees: The state requires a license to carry a concealed handgun on one's person or in a vehicle. The sheriff of a person's home county issues such permits to qualified persons 21 years or older for four year terms. Oregon will only grant licenses to nonresidents who live in bordering states and express a viable need for concealed carry in Oregon. Such permits are issued at the discretion of any local sheriff. Oregon does not recognize carry permits issued by other states. But Oregon permittees enjoy the freedom to carry in most public areas.

Persons without Oregon permits: A loaded handgun may be carried in a vehicle if it is in a visible belt holster. But any handgun that is readily accessible and hidden from view is prohibited. This would include guns kept in unlocked glove compartments, console boxes and under one's seat. Handguns secured in cases and stowed in the trunk are legitimate. If a vehicle has no trunk, a handgun may be kept in a *locked* glove compartment or console box as long as the key is not inserted in the lock. Carrying a concealed handgun in a motorcycle, ATV or snowmobile requires that the gun be either trigger locked or in a locked container.

Long guns may be loaded and carried openly in gun racks. They may also be secured in a closed gun case or vehicle trunk as long as the weapons are not concealed upon the person.

Oregon's preemption law allows localities to regulate the public carry of *loaded* firearms. Portland and other cities require all firearms carried in a public setting or private vehicle to be unloaded and in plain view or securely cased unless the person has an Oregon license. And state law prohibits open carry by non-permittees in any "public building." This would include K-12 schools, colleges, hospitals, the state capitol and any local or state government offices.

All Persons: Oregon allows anyone in a recreational vehicle to possess a loaded, concealed handgun without a permit while the RV is parked in a campsite and being utilized as a residence. But vehicle carry laws apply when the RV is on the road. And Oregon prohibits all gun possession in court facilities and racecourses.

Pennsylvania

Total prohibition *(+0, good carry privileges for permittees, but non-permittees need help)* **Total freedom**

0 ------- 10 ------- 20 ------- 30 ------- 40 ------- 50 ------- 60 ------- 70 ------- 80 ------ 90 ------ 100

^

CHECKLIST

- ***Standard firearms & ammo:** no permit required for possession or sale – see p.3
- ***Semi-auto guns & high capacity magazines:** no permit required for possession or sale
- ***Machine guns & suppressors:** ownership lawful per federal law compliance
- ***Firearm law uniformity:** preemption law, firearm laws uniform throughout state
- ***Right of Self-Defense:** NRA-model castle doctrine, *stand your ground* in public areas
- ***Open carry:** unrestricted under state law in most public areas
- ***Licensed concealed carry:** licenses issued on a "shall issue" basis to residents and nonresidents
- ***Constitutional or "no permit required" concealed carry:** no
- ***Out-of-state permit recognition:** automatic recognition for *vehicle carry* of handguns by nonresidents w/ out-of-state permits; conditional recognition for on-foot carry (see p.65)
- ***Weapons allowed for *licensed* carry:** limited to handguns and certain NFA registered weapons

VEHICLES

- ***Vehicle carry by non-permittees:** handguns must be unloaded and securely locked in the vehicle trunk or rear storage area; rifles and shotguns must be unloaded and may be in the passenger compartment but should be cased
- ***Vehicle gun possession at colleges:** subject to college administrative policy
- ***Vehicle gun possession at K-12 schools:** gun possession prohibited; but legal defenses exist
- ***Duty to notify LEO of permit status:** upon demand of police officer
- ***RV carry while "boondocking":** parking lot owners may restrict gun carry by visitors – see p.8

- ***State Parks:** concealed handgun carry by recognized licensees permitted
- ***Restaurants serving alcohol:** permittees may carry while eating in dining areas – see p.3
- ***Hotels:** subject to hotel policy enforcement – see p.7
- ***Airports:** carry allowed in non-sterile terminal areas and parking lots – see p.9

Travelers to Pennsylvania will find the state to have an even mix of urban and rural character. This contributes to a legal dichotomy where gun ownership is both respected and, in certain instances, heavily encumbered. A famous pundit once described Pennsylvania as a state where, "Philadelphia is on one side, Pittsburgh is on the other, and Alabama is in the middle."

Recognized permittees: The state requires a license to carry a loaded handgun in a vehicle or concealed on or about one's person. The sheriff of a resident's home county issues such permits to persons 21 years or older for five year terms. Any sheriff's office may also issue a license to a nonresident who possesses a permit from his home state. But recent reports indicate only certain sheriffs are actually accepting applications from nonresidents. Any nonresident with a valid, out-of-state permit may carry a loaded handgun in his vehicle so long as he restricts his transport to the vehicle's interior. Concealed carry outside one's vehicle requires a license recognized by the Attorney General (see p. 65). Permittees may carry in most public areas except K-12 schools, the state capitol and mental hospitals.

Persons without recognized permits: Vehicle carry of any firearm by an unlicensed individual is strictly regulated. Handguns must be unloaded, cased and secured in the trunk or rear storage area. The weapons should also be separated from any ammunition. Travelers should be enroute to a vacation dwelling, gun range or residence unless they have a permit.

Open carry of a loaded handgun while on foot is allowed in most public areas. The weapon should be secured in a visible belt holster and the carrier may not enter a vehicle with the gun. The state's preemption law prevents localities from regulating any aspect of this carry mode. And most police are aware of the legal basis for open carry. But travelers should note that handgun carry within Philadelphia is limited to persons possessing valid, recognized licenses.

All Persons: Rifles and shotguns must be unloaded and should be secured in commercial cases or gun racks. Long guns may be transported in the passenger compartment but should remain unloaded regardless of whether a person possesses a carry permit. Licensed firearms carry only applies to handguns and certain short-barreled shotguns & rifles registered under the National Firearms Act.

Peter J Cesnakas & Associates

Rhode Island

Total prohibition *(+0, gun owners face some rough waves in the "Ocean state")* **Total freedom**

0 ------- 10 ------- 20 ------- 30 ------- 40 ------- 50 ------- 60 ------- 70 ------- 80 ------ 90 ------ 100

^

CHECKLIST

***Standard firearms & ammo:** no permit required for possession or sale – see p.3
***Semi-auto guns & high capacity magazines:** no permit required for possession or sale
***Machine guns & suppressors:** personal ownership prohibited; bump stocks prohibited
***Firearm law uniformity:** preemption law, firearm laws uniform throughout state
***Right of Self-Defense:** no NRA-model castle doctrine, *duty to retreat* in public areas
***Open carry:** prohibited in all public areas unless one has an attorney general-issued permit
***Licensed concealed carry:** licenses issued on a discretionary basis to residents & nonresidents
***Constitutional or "no permit required" concealed carry:** no
***Out-of-state permit recognition:** no general recognition, some *limited* recognition (see below)
***Weapons allowed for *licensed* carry:** limited to handguns only

VEHICLES

Vehicle carry by non-permittees:** a carry permit issued by any state or locality is required for transportation of handguns ***through the state, otherwise McClure-Volkmer p.5 applies; unloaded rifles and shotguns may be transported without a permit in a vehicle
***Vehicle gun possession at colleges:** subject to college administrative policy
***Vehicle gun possession at K-12 schools:** firearm possession prohibited by RI DOE policy, but statutory exception (currently overridden by this policy) still exists for state permittees
***Duty to notify LEO of permit status:** upon demand of police officer
***RV carry while "boondocking":** parking lot owners may restrict gun carry by visitors – see p.8

***State Parks:** firearms carry prohibited; firearms must be unloaded and cased in vehicle
***Restaurants serving alcohol:** permittees may carry while eating in dining areas – see p.3
***Hotels:** statutory allowance for guest rejection or ejectment for gun possession – see p.7
***Airports:** carry allowed in non-sterile terminal areas and parking lots – see p.9

Rhode Island's handgun carry laws reflect the restrictive attitude evident along much of the Northeast Coast. Carry is limited to those with enough political influence to acquire a permit. Everyone else must surrender their personal protection rights when they exit the front door.

Recognized permittees: The state requires a license to carry a handgun about one's person or in a vehicle. The police chief of an applicant's hometown issues such licenses for a four-year term. Nonresidents with carry permits from other states may apply to any city's police chief for a Rhode Island permit. The attorney general will also issue permits to nonresidents but will not require the possession of another state's permit. Applicants must be at least 21 years or older and be able to articulate a "proper reason" to carry a handgun. This statutory language has prompted some authorities to exercise discretion over what is supposed to be a "shall issue" standard at the local level.

Rhode Island will recognize any carry permit issued by another state or locality if the traveler restricts the transport of the handgun to his vehicle's interior (sec.11-47-8). He must also be passing through the state on a continuous journey with no intention of staying for any period. This would mean that even a one-day vacation within Rhode Island would not be allowed under this exception.

Persons without recognized permits: A handgun may only be transported in a vehicle if the weapon is unloaded, secured in a gun case and the ammunition is stowed in the trunk or outside storage compartment. If the vehicle has no trunk, the ammunition must be locked in a separate container. One must also be traveling between their home and business or going to or from a gun shop, gunsmith, repair facility or target range unless they can qualify as a traveler on a "through journey" (see p.5).

All Persons: Any person may transport rifles and shotguns in a vehicle as long as the weapons are unloaded. Rhode Island does not require that the firearms be cased or secured in any specific way. But, due to the state's restrictive attitude toward handgun possession, travelers should exercise caution in this area by securing their long guns in commercial gun cases or trunk mounted gun racks. Transport modes such as these will be viewed much more favorably by East Coast police officers not accustomed to firearms carry by citizens.

South Carolina

Total prohibition ***(+0, good state, but reciprocity & open carry options could be better)*** **Total freedom**

0 ------- 10 ------- 20 ------- 30 ------- 40 ------- 50 ------- 60 ------- 70 ------- 80 ------ 90 ------ 100

^

CHECKLIST

- ***Standard firearms & ammo:** no permit required for possession or sale – see p.3
- ***Semi-auto guns & high capacity magazines:** no permit required for possession or sale
- ***Machine guns or suppressors:** ownership lawful per federal law compliance
- ***Firearm law uniformity:** preemption law, firearm laws uniform throughout state
- ***Right of Self-Defense:** NRA-model castle doctrine, *stand your ground* in public areas
- ***Open carry:** prohibited in most public areas
- ***Licensed concealed carry:** licenses issued on a "shall issue" basis to residents and nonresidents
- ***Constitutional or "no permit required" concealed carry:** no
- ***Out-of-state permit recognition:** conditional recognition of permits from other states (see p. 65)
- ***Weapons allowed for *licensed* carry:** limited to handguns only

VEHICLES

- ***Vehicle carry by non-permittees:** loaded handguns may be carried in a closed glove compartment, console box or trunk; rifles and shotguns may be loaded while in the trunk or passenger area (some exceptions - see below)
- ***Vehicle gun possession at colleges:** permittees lawful; must be in *closed* compartment
- ***Vehicle gun possession at K-12 schools:** South Carolina permittee w/loaded handgun secured in *closed* glove compartment, console box or trunk lawful
- ***Duty to notify LEO of permit status:** immediately upon official contact
- ***RV carry while "boondocking":** parking lot owners may restrict gun carry by visitors – see p.8

- ***State Parks:** concealed handgun carry by recognized licensees permitted
- ***Restaurants serving alcohol:** permittees may carry while eating in dining areas – see p.3
- ***Hotels:** statutory allowance for guest rejection & "force of law" posting prohibitions – see p.7
- ***Airports:** carry prohibited if terminal is "publicly-owned"; car carry O.K. for permittees – see p.9

South Carolina's "southern" flavor for firearms is reflected in its laws. A healthy respect for private gun ownership coupled with some very positive jurisprudence ensures a pleasant journey for most while visiting the birthplace of the Confederacy.

Recognized permittees: South Carolina requires a license to carry a concealed handgun on or about one's person. Permits are issued to residents who are at least 21 years old for 5-year terms. A qualified nonresident who owns real property within the state is also eligible for a permit. Permits from other states are recognized as long as that state requires permittees to pass a criminal background check and gun safety course. The out-of-state permittee must be a resident of the state where the permit was issued and may only use his permit for *concealed* handgun carry. In a vehicle, this would include on his person, under the seat, or in any open or closed compartment. When approached by a police officer, he must inform the officer that he is carrying a concealed handgun with a permit. Recognized permittees may carry in most areas except scholastic athletic events, medical & day care facilities, govt. meetings, buses, churches and all private businesses & special events that post against carry.

Persons without recognized permits: A loaded handgun may be carried in a vehicle if it is contained in a closed glove compartment, console box, or trunk. A motorcycle rider may secure his loaded handgun in a closed saddlebag or similar accessory container.

Handgun carry on foot is restricted to certain specific conditions. Generally, the weapon must be unloaded and secured in a package or closed case. A loaded handgun may be carried from a vehicle to a hotel room so long as its owner has paid the rent and the hotel tax. Licensed hunters and fishermen may also carry loaded handguns while engaged in hunting or fishing.

All Persons: Vehicle carry of loaded rifles and shotguns is lawful unless traveling to a state park, recreational area or a wildlife area during hunting season. All long guns must then be unloaded and secured in cases. Schools, universities & the state capitol are off-limits to gun possession unless one is a permittee and his handgun is secured in a closed compartment of his locked vehicle. Any gun possession on public transportation (buses) or inside publicly-owned buildings (except rest areas) is also prohibited.

South Dakota

Total prohibition *(+2, snowmobile & ATV carry no longer requires a permit)* **Total freedom**

0 ------- 10 ------- 20 ------- 30 ------- 40 ------- 50 ------- 60 ------- 70 ------- 80 ------ 90 ------ 100

^

CHECKLIST

- ***Standard firearms & ammo:** no permit required for possession or sale – see p.3
- ***Semi-auto guns & high capacity magazines:** no permit required for possession or sale
- ***Machine guns & suppressors:** ownership lawful per federal law compliance
- ***Firearm law uniformity:** preemption law, civil penalties & A.G. prosecution for local violations
- ***Right of Self-Defense:** NRA-model castle doctrine, *stand your ground* in public areas
- ***Open carry:** unrestricted under state law in most public areas
- ***Licensed concealed carry:** licenses issued on a "shall issue" basis to residents only
- ***Constitutional or "no permit required" concealed carry:** yes – see below
- ***Out-of-state permit recognition:** automatic recognition for all non-residents with carry permits
- ***Weapons allowed for *licensed* carry:** limited to handguns only

VEHICLES

- ***Vehicle carry by non-permittees:** loaded firearms may be carried anywhere in a vehicle
- ***Vehicle gun possession at colleges:** subject to college administrative policy
- ***Vehicle gun possession at K-12 schools:** gun possession prohibited except at nonpublic schools
- ***Duty to notify LEO of permit/carry status:** upon demand of police officer
- ***RV carry while "boondocking":** parking lot owners may restrict gun carry by visitors – see p.8

- ***State Parks:** concealed handgun carry by recognized licensees permitted
- ***Restaurants serving alcohol:** permittees may carry while eating in dining areas – see p.3
- ***Hotels:** subject to hotel policy enforcement – see p.7
- ***Airports:** carry allowed in non-sterile terminal areas and parking lots – see p.9

The 1960s witnessed a large influx of workers into South Dakota. Aside from boosting the local economy, these new arrivals participated in one of the most crucial defense projects of the post-war era. They were tasked with constructing hundreds of missile silos for the newly developed Minuteman ICBMs. These missiles were aptly named after the farmers who took on the British in 1775 Boston. But their presence also reflected the commitment South Dakota has always had for the values that make this country great. With the state's 2019 enactment of "permitless carry", South Dakota continues this tradition by advancing gun rights to its logical apex.

Recognized permittees: Licenses are issued to carry concealed handguns on one's person or in one's vehicle. Such permits are valid for 5 years and are only granted through county sheriffs to residents who are 18 years or older. South Dakota also offers *enhanced* permits to residents 21 and older that are valid for 5 years and offer the applicant better options for reciprocity when traveling.

South Dakota will recognize any out-of-state permit held by a non-resident. Licensed concealed carry is lawful in most public areas except the prohibited areas in "All Persons" – (see below).

Persons without recognized permits: A license is not required to carry a concealed, loaded handgun in a vehicle or on foot. The state recently enacted permitless carry. So, while licenses (both regular and enhanced) are still issued to residents, they are not required for carry within the state.

Open carry of a loaded handgun on foot is allowed under most circumstances and more commonly practiced in the state's rural areas. South Dakota's preemption law prevents localities from regulating most aspects of gun carry, possession and transport. And recent amendments to the law provide for civil penalties and attorney general action against localities that violate it.

All Persons: Vehicle carry of loaded rifles and shotguns is generally unregulated. Such weapons may be carried anywhere, including the passenger compartment. But all long guns should be secured in cases when passing through a game preserve or wildlife refuge. Motorcycle and snowmobile riders may now carry loaded firearms without possessing recognized permits.

And gun possession is prohibited to everyone in K-12 public schools, bars, courthouses & the state capitol. A recent law change now allows gun carry at *nonpublic* K-12 schools (*permittees only* per federal law). And those possessing enhanced permits issued by South Dakota may carry concealed handguns in the state capitol if they provide notice to the state Highway Patrol at least 24 hours prior to any visit.

Tennessee

Total prohibition *(+0, Guns & the Grand Ole Opry – nothin' says Tennessee better!)* **Total freedom**

0 ------- 10 ------- 20 ------- 30 ------- 40 ------- 50 ------- 60 ------- 70 ------- 80 ------ 90 ------ 100

^

CHECKLIST

***Standard firearms & ammo:** no permit required for possession or sale – see p.3
***Semi-auto guns & high capacity magazines:** no permit required for possession or sale
***Machine guns & suppressors:** ownership lawful per federal law compliance
***Firearm law uniformity:** preemption law, gun laws uniform; localities may be sued for violations
***Right of Self-Defense:** NRA-model castle doctrine, *stand your ground* in public areas
***Open carry:** prohibited unless one possesses a recognized permit to carry a handgun
***Licensed concealed carry:** licenses issued on a "shall issue" basis to residents and nonresidents
***Constitutional or "no permit required" concealed carry:** no
***Out-of-state permit recognition:** automatic recognition of all nonresidents with carry permits
***Weapons allowed for *licensed* carry:** limited to handguns only

VEHICLES

***Vehicle carry by non-permittees:** loaded firearms may be carried anywhere in a motor vehicle or boat (glove compartment, console box, gun case, etc.)
***Vehicle gun possession at colleges:** lawful for permittees, code enforcement preempted
***Vehicle gun possession at K-12 schools:** Tennessee permittee w/loaded handgun lawful
***Duty to notify LEO of permit status:** upon demand of police officer
***RV carry while "boondocking":** parking lot owners may *not* prohibit permittees w/guns – p.8

***State Parks:** concealed handgun carry by recognized licensees permitted
***Restaurants serving alcohol:** permittees may carry while eating in dining areas – see p.3
***Hotels:** statutory allowance for guest rejection & "force of law" posting prohibitions – see p.7
***Airports:** carry allowed in non-sterile terminal areas & parking lots unless posted – see p. 9

Alvin York's birthplace has greatly improved for gun owners in recent years. This fact, along with a solid tradition of private gun ownership, will provide most travelers with a very pleasant visit.

Recognized permittees: A license is required to carry a loaded handgun either openly or concealed. Permits (now referred to as "enhanced") are issued to residents who are 21 years or older for 8-year terms or for life. "Concealed carry only" permits are also issued to residents for 5 year terms. These licenses require less training but have more restrictions as to where and how you can carry. Tennessee recognizes any out-of-state carry permit as long as the permittee is not a resident of Tennessee and restricts his carry to handguns only. Nonresidents will be issued 8-year permits only if they are *regularly employed* in the state. Most areas off-limits to carry, such as schools, colleges, civic centers & public recreation buildings, are posted with signage. In some areas such as public meetings, the signs may prohibit all firearms carry or allow "concealed carry only" by permittees. These prohibitions can include all property owned by the entity. "Open areas," such as local parks & campgrounds, are lawful unless a school-sponsored activity is occurring in the immediate vicinity. Then permittee carry is not allowed.

Tennessee prohibits parking lot owners from preventing permittees from storing firearms in their locked vehicles as long as the guns remain hidden from view. In addition, employers may not take adverse action against employee-permittees who keep guns in their vehicles while in compliance with this law.

Persons without recognized permits: A non-permittee is prohibited from carrying firearms with the "intent to go armed." This would include any weapons that are loaded and carried on his person while on foot, unless he is engaged in hunting, sport shooting or other gun-related activity. This prevents any open carry of a handgun without a recognized permit.

But a recent law change allows an exception for vehicle carry. Anyone in lawful possession of firearms may carry them loaded anywhere in a motor vehicle or boat. The weapons may be in the glove compartment, console box, trunk, under the seat or secured in commercial gun cases.

All Persons: Tennessee preempts localities from regulating most aspects of firearm possession, carry or transport and also provides for civil actions against cities that violate this standard. But even with this strengthened law, some contradictory signage may still exist.

Texas

Total prohibition ***(+0, Lone Star lives up to its reputation when it comes to guns)*** **Total freedom**

0 ------- 10 ------- 20 ------- 30 ------ 40 ------- 50 ------- 60 ------- 70 ------- 80 ------- 90 ------ 100

^

CHECKLIST

***Standard firearms & ammo:** no permit required for possession or sale – see p.3
***Semi-auto guns & high capacity magazines:** no permit required for possession or sale
***Machine guns & suppressors:** ownership lawful per federal law compliance
***Firearm law uniformity:** preemption statute, firearm laws uniform throughout state
***Right of Self-Defense:** NRA-model castle doctrine, *stand your ground* in public areas
***Open carry:** prohibited in all public areas unless handgun is holstered and one is a permittee
***Licensed concealed carry:** licenses issued on a "shall issue" basis to residents and nonresidents
***Constitutional or "no permit required" concealed carry:** no
***Out-of-state permit recognition:** conditional recognition of permits from other states (see p. 65)
***Weapons allowed for *licensed* carry:** limited to handguns only

VEHICLES

***Vehicle carry by non-permittees:** *concealed*, loaded handguns may be carried anywhere in a vehicle; loaded long guns (concealed or plain view) may be carried anywhere
***Vehicle gun possession at colleges:** lawful for permittees and their firearms
***Vehicle gun possession at K-12 schools:** Texas permittee w/loaded handgun lawful
***Duty to notify LEO of permit status:** immediately upon official contact (ID request)
***RV carry while "boondocking":** parking lot owners may restrict gun carry by visitors – see p.8

***State Parks:** concealed handgun carry by recognized licensees permitted
***Restaurant serving alcohol:** permittees may carry while eating in dining areas – see p.3
***Hotels:** "force of law" posting prohibitions; hotels must post gun policies on reservations – see p.7
***Airports:** carry allowed in non-sterile terminal areas unless posted; car carry in parking lots O.K.

Travelers to the Lone Star State will find its reputation as a gun owner's paradise to be rightly deserved. And despite adjusting its frontier laws to fit the demands of a modern society, Texas still embodies the gun loving spirit of native sons Audie Murphy and Sam Houston.

Recognized permittees: Licenses to carry a handgun on or about one's person are issued by DPS to residents who are 21 years or older for an initial term of 4 years and a subsequent renewal term of 5 years. Texas will also issue permits to nonresidents and will recognize permittees from states whose laws mandate background checks of their licensees. A permittee must be at least 21, carry his handgun concealed or, if carried openly, in a shoulder or belt holster, and inform any policeman who requests his ID that he has a carry license. Places off-limits to carry include bars, courts, polling places, racetracks, schools, colleges (*concealed* carry O.K. w/restrictions), & sporting events. Hospitals, nursing homes, amusement parks & govt. meetings are off-limits if posted. Handguns secured in vehicles in parking lots for all these areas are lawful unless a school-sponsored activity is occurring within the lot. And any business or church may post its property against open or concealed carry with approved signage.

Persons without recognized permit: A handgun may not be carried "on or about one's person" while on foot. This would include any readily accessible handgun (concealed or open) within arm's reach. Texas exempts persons who are traveling as well as sportsmen involved in lawful firearm activity such as hunting and target shooting. These exemptions apply while a person is actually engaged in these pursuits.

Vehicle carry of a loaded handgun is allowed if the weapon is kept concealed and the person carrying the weapon is not involved in any criminal activity (except routine traffic violations). This "traveling presumption" allows anyone to carry concealed, loaded handguns anywhere in their motor vehicles or watercrafts.

All Persons: Loaded long guns may be carried anywhere in a vehicle including, but not limited to, gun cases, trunks and window racks. Texas law prevents local regulation of this and other gun rights and also forbids landlords from restricting lawful gun possession on their premises.

Any recreational vehicle being used as living quarters is considered one's home where legal prohibitions on loaded handgun carry do not apply. And hotels are required to inform their guests of any firearm-related policies prior to reservation or face legal sanctions.

Utah

Total prohibition ***(+0, Mormon sensibility & frontier toughness make for good gun laws)*** **Total freedom**

0 ------- 10 ------- 20 ------- 30 ------- 40 ------- 50 ------- 60 ------- 70 ------- 80 ------ 90 ------ 100

^

CHECKLIST

***Standard firearms & ammo:** no permit required for possession or sale – see p.3
***Semi-auto guns & high capacity magazines:** no permit required for possession or sale
***Machine guns & suppressors:** ownership lawful per federal law compliance
***Firearm law uniformity:** preemption statute, firearm laws uniform throughout state
***Right of Self-Defense:** NRA-model castle doctrine, *stand your ground* in public areas
***Open carry:** "loaded" carry by non-permittees prohibited in most public areas (see below)
***Licensed concealed carry:** licenses issued on a "shall issue" basis to residents and nonresidents
***Constitutional or "no permit required" concealed carry:** no
***Out-of-state permit recognition:** automatic recognition of carry permits from all other states
***Weapons allowed for *licensed* carry:** include any lawful firearm

VEHICLES

***Vehicle carry by non-permittees:** rifles and shotguns must be unloaded; handguns may be loaded and carried anywhere in a vehicle
***Vehicle gun possession at colleges:** lawful for any gun owner, some code enforcement
***Vehicle gun possession at K-12 schools:** Utah permittee w/loaded handgun lawful
***Duty to notify LEO of permit status:** upon demand of police officer
***RV carry while "boondocking":** most parking areas O.K.; churches & govt. may restrict – p.8

***State Parks:** concealed handgun carry by recognized licensees permitted
***Restaurants serving alcohol:** permittees may carry while eating in dining areas – see p.3
***Hotels:** statutory allowance for guest rejection or ejectment for gun possession – see p.7
***Airports:** carry allowed in non-sterile terminal areas & parking lots – see p. 9

Utah was founded more than a century ago by hardy Mormon pioneers who relied heavily upon firearms for survival. The gun-wielding advantage of these early settlers decided many a battle with Indians and other hostiles. Modern Utah reflects this frontier heritage in its user-friendly gun laws.

Recognized permittees: The state issues a license to carry a concealed firearm on one's person or in a vehicle. The license allows for the carry of any firearm, not just a handgun, and is issued by the Bureau of Criminal Identification to qualified persons 21 years or older for a 5-year term (provisional licenses for 18-20 year olds are also available). Utah grants licenses to both residents and non-residents and recognizes any valid, out-of-state carry permit. A recognized permittee may carry a concealed firearm in all public places except secure areas (marked with signage or security screenings), houses of worship and private residences that post notices. Utah is one of the few states that allow resident permittees to carry in primary & secondary schools.

Persons without recognized permits: Loaded handguns may be carried anywhere in a vehicle. Under one's seat, in a glove compartment or within a console box is legitimate as long as the vehicle is in the gun owner's lawful possession. The owner must also be eighteen years of age or older.

Utah does not allow the carry of "loaded" firearms on public streets and posted prohibited areas by non-permittees while on foot. But Utah defines "loaded" to only include chamber-loaded semi-autos. So a non-permittee could openly carry a magazine loaded, chamber unloaded pistol and still be O.K. in *most* public areas. Utah preempts local regulation of carry issues.

All Persons: Any traveler, regardless of permit status, may carry long guns in the passenger compartment of his vehicle as long as the weapons remain unloaded. Utah law deems rifles and shotguns to be unloaded when their firing chambers contain no "live" rounds. The weapons' magazines may contain ammunition. Muzzle-loading firearms are loaded when capped or primed. Long guns may be kept in window-mounted gun racks, commercial gun cases or any convenient place for stowage.

Most property owners are prohibited from enforcing "no guns in vehicles" policies in their parking lots if the firearms remain locked in one's vehicle and secured from view. Government entities, churches and single-family homes are exempt from this provision. And K-12 schools are subject to the general law governing firearm possession on school grounds.

Vermont

Total prohibition *(+0, despite an influx of granola-eaters, gun laws are good - for now)* **Total freedom**

0 ------- 10 ------- 20 ------- 30 ------- 40 ------- 50 ------- 60 ------- 70 ------- 80 ------ 90 ------ 100

^

CHECKLIST

*__Standard firearms & ammo:__ no permit required for possession or sale – see p.3

*__Semi-auto guns & high capacity magazines:__ possession & sale of over 10 shot long gun mags & over 15 shot pistol mags prohibited – some exceptions - see below

*__Machine guns & suppressors:__ lawful per federal law compliance; bump stocks prohibited

*__Firearm law uniformity:__ preemption statute, firearm laws uniform throughout state

*__Right of Self-Defense:__ no NRA-model castle doctrine; *duty to retreat* in public places

*__Open carry:__ unrestricted in most public areas and generally accepted

*__Licensed concealed carry:__ no licenses issued for concealed carry (license not required)

*__Constitutional or "no permit required" concealed carry:__ yes – see below

*__Out-of-state permit recognition:__ no official recognition needed – permit not required to carry

*__Weapons allowed for *licensed* carry:__ not applicable – no licenses issued

VEHICLES

*__Vehicle carry for all persons:__ rifles and shotguns carried in a vehicle must be unloaded; handguns may be carried loaded and concealed anywhere in the vehicle

*__Vehicle gun possession at colleges:__ subject to college administrative policy

*__Vehicle gun possession at K-12 schools:__ unloaded firearms locked in cases lawful; per federal law, loaded handgun carry would require Vermont-issued permit; no such permit exists; therefore loaded carry would be illegal under the Gun Free School Zones Act

*__Duty to notify LEO of permit/carry status:__ N/A – permits not issued by state

*__RV carry while "boondocking":__ parking lot owners may restrict gun carry by visitors – see p.8

*__State Parks:__ concealed handgun carry by any non-felon permitted

*__Restaurants serving alcohol:__ any non-felon may carry while eating in dining areas

*__Hotels:__ subject to hotel policy enforcement & "force of law" posting prohibitions – see p.7

*__Airports:__ carry allowed in non-sterile terminal areas & parking lots – see p. 9

Vermont is a proudly independent state whose laws have always reflected the values of its colonial heritage. And while current gun laws in the state are comparatively good, the recent influx of native New Yorkers has caused some definite concern. 2018 witnessed the passage of the state's first major gun control initiative in years. This legislation not only created a qualified ban on magazines and bump stocks, it could also signal the beginning of some hard times ahead for Vermont's gun owners.

Vermont does not require a license to carry a firearm. Persons may carry loaded handguns concealed or openly almost anywhere in the state. Vehicle carry is viewed in the same light as any other carry. A concealed, loaded handgun placed in a glove compartment, console box or briefcase is legitimate. A pistol carried directly on the person is also O.K. as long as the weapon is not carried with the avowed purpose of injuring someone.

Rifles and shotguns in a vehicle may be transported openly or secured in commercial gun cases. But due to conservation laws, long guns must be unloaded while in a vehicle.

Vermont prohibits firearms carry in courthouses, school buildings, and on the grounds of any "state institution." This would generally include facilities such as prisons and mental hospitals as well as most buildings leased or owned by the state government and under the control of the Dept. of Bldgs. (excluding colleges and universities). State Historic sites and highway rest areas limit carry to concealed firearms only.

Vermont also prohibits possession of high capacity magazines (long gun magazines over 10 shots & handgun magazines over 15 shots) and "bump stocks." Those magazines lawfully possessed prior to April 11, 2018, are exempt from prohibition as are any newly produced magazines being used by out-of-state residents for official shooting competitions held in the state. Any attached tubular magazines for .22 rimfire guns are also O.K. But high-capacity mags not fitting into an exemption are banned from possession, sale, transfer or import.

Vermont has a preemption law that prevents municipalities from enacting laws that regulate the carry, possession or sale of firearms. Cities may still control the discharge and use of firearms. But travelers can expect uniformity throughout the state with the firearm laws that most directly affect them.

Virginia

Total prohibition *(-8, weakened preemption & red flag laws signal rough times ahead)* **Total freedom**

0 ------- 10 ------- 20 ------- 30 ------- 40 ------- 50 ------- 60 ------- 70 ------- 80 ------ 90 ------ 100

^

CHECKLIST

- ***Standard firearms & ammo:** no permit required for possession or sale – see p.3
- ***Semi-auto guns & high capacity magazines:** "streetsweeper"-style shotguns & bump stocks prohibited – over 20 shot mags prohibited to nonpermittees in certain urban public areas
- ***Machine guns & suppressors:** state registration required of machine gun ownership; suppressor ownership lawful per federal law compliance
- ***Firearm law uniformity:** preemption statute, but localities may regulate carry in many public areas; some counties may also restrict *loaded* long guns in vehicles
- ***Right of Self-Defense:** no NRA castle doctrine, *stand your ground* in public not codified
- ***Open carry:** unrestricted under state law, but localities may regulate in some public areas – see below
- ***Licensed concealed carry:** licenses issued on a "shall issue" basis to residents and nonresidents
- ***Constitutional or "no permit required" concealed carry:** no
- ***Out-of-state permit recognition:** automatic recognition of carry permits from all other states
- ***Weapons allowed for *licensed* carry:** limited to handguns only

VEHICLES

- ***Vehicle carry by non-permittees:** loaded handguns may be carried in plain view or secured in the glove compartment or console box; rifles and shotguns may be kept in gun cases in the rear of the passenger compartment or trunk (for loaded long guns - see "all persons")
- ***Vehicle gun possession at colleges:** college regulation through VA's administrative code
- ***Vehicle gun possession at K-12 schools:** Virginia permittee w/loaded handgun lawful; handgun should be unloaded and cased if permittee leaves vehicle
- ***Duty to notify LEO of permit status:** upon demand of police officer
- ***RV carry while "boondocking":** parking lot owners may restrict gun carry by visitors – see p.8

- ***State Parks:** concealed handgun carry by recognized licensees permitted
- ***Restaurants serving alcohol:** permittees may carry while eating in dining areas – see p.3
- ***Hotels:** subject to hotel policy enforcement – see p.7
- ***Airports:** carry prohibited in passenger terminals; parking lots O.K. unless posted – see p. 9

The birthplace of many of America's founders historically displayed a healthy respect for gun rights. But recent election results in the Old Dominion could signal tough times for gun owners. Demographic changes make Virginia the "front and center" in the battle to preserve the 2nd amendment.

Recognized permittees: Virginia requires a license to carry a handgun concealed about the person. Such permits are issued to both residents (through local circuit court) and nonresidents (through state police) for 5-year terms. Virginia recognizes permits from all other states as long as the permittee is at least 21 years old, possesses a state-issued photo ID, and did not previously have a Virginia permit issued to him revoked. Carry is lawful in most public areas except churches (if posted), courthouses, airports, private businesses that ban carry, executive & legislative branch offices w/ posted signage, K-12 schools & sponsored event, most colleges & universities and public bldgs., parks & parades where carry is prohibited by local ordinance.

Persons without recognized permits: A loaded handgun may be carried in a vehicle if the weapon is in plain view or secured in a container or vehicle compartment. "Vehicle compartment" would include a glove compartment, console box or trunk. A loaded handgun could also be kept in a briefcase or similar container situated anywhere in the vehicle, including about one's person. "Container carry" applies only to handguns.

Open carry is allowed but may be subject to restrictions by local ordinance. And the state still prohibits non-permittees from carrying loaded center-fire firearms with capacities greater than 20 rounds in many urban areas.

All Persons: Localities may prohibit carry in parks & buildings they control as well as any permitted outdoor event such as a parade or demonstration. Postings must be present or the prohibition is unenforceable.

Long guns in vehicles are lawful if they are cased and stowed in the trunk or rear storage area. Long guns must remain unloaded on Dept. of Natural Resources property (conservation & wildlife management areas) and National Forest lands. And some counties may require long guns to be unloaded unless the guns are possessed for "personal safety" reasons in the course of one's employment.

Washington

Total prohibition *(-3, firearms carry prohibited in day care centers)* **Total freedom**

0 ------- 10 ------- 20 ------- 30 ------- 40 ------- 50 ------- 60 ------- 70 ------- 80 ------ 90 ------ 100

^

CHECKLIST

*__Standard firearms & ammo:__ no permit required for possession or sale by individuals – see p. 3
*__Semi-auto guns & high capacity magazines:__ "assault rifles" restricted to those 21 & older
*__Machine guns & suppressors:__ personal ownership of machine guns & bump stocks prohibited; suppressor ownership lawful per federal law compliance;
*__Firearm law uniformity:__ preemption statute, firearm laws uniform throughout state
*__Right of Self-Defense:__ no NRA castle doctrine, *stand your ground* in public not codified
*__Open carry:__ unrestricted under state law in most public areas
*__Licensed concealed carry:__ licenses issued on a "shall issue" basis to residents and nonresidents
*__Constitutional or "no permit required" concealed carry:__ no
*__Out-of-state permit recognition:__ conditional recognition of permits from other states (see p. 65)
*__Weapons allowed for *licensed* carry:__ limited to handguns only

VEHICLES

*__Vehicle carry by non-permittees:__ handguns must be unloaded and secured in commercial gun cases; long guns must be unloaded
*__Vehicle gun possession at colleges:__ prohibitions enforced through WA's admin. code
*__Vehicle gun possession at K-12 schools:__ Washington permittee w/loaded handgun lawful while picking up or dropping off a student
*__Duty to notify LEO of permit status:__ upon demand of police officer
*__RV carry while "boondocking":__ parking lot owners may restrict gun carry by visitors – see p.8

*__State Parks:__ concealed handgun carry by recognized licensees permitted
*__Restaurants serving alcohol:__ permittees may carry while eating in dining areas – see p.3
*__Hotels:__ subject to hotel policy enforcement – see p.7
*__Airports:__ carry allowed in non-sterile terminal areas & parking lots unless posted – see p. 9

Washington's vast tracts of wilderness create a setting where gun ownership is quite common. Despite the recent passage of laws restricting the purchase of certain firearms, the state's carry laws still reflect more Rocky Mountain than Pacific coast.

Recognized permittees: A license is required to carry a loaded handgun concealed on one's person or in any personal vehicle or public transportation. Residents are issued permits through their local police or sheriff. Nonresidents may apply in person to any local law enforcement agency. Licenses are valid for 5 years. Washington recognizes permits from states that recognize Washington, require fingerprint-based background checks of their licensees and do not issue permits to persons under 21. A recognized permittee must be a nonresident and is limited to handgun carry only. He must also keep the weapon locked up and concealed from view if it is left in his vehicle. Carry is prohibited in courtrooms, bars, K-12 schools, day care centers, mental health facilities, horse racetracks, outdoor music festivals and many colleges.

Persons without recognized permits: Loaded handguns may not be carried anywhere in a vehicle. They must be unloaded and secured in gun cases specifically designed for handguns. Loaded magazines may be carried in the vehicle as long as they are not inserted into any handgun.

While on foot, a non-permittee may carry a loaded, concealed handgun while engaged in outdoor activities such as hunting, fishing, camping, and target shooting. Open carry of a loaded handgun is legitimate and best practiced by securing the weapon in a visible belt holster. Washington's preemption law prevents most local regulation of this carry mode. But along with the prohibited areas listed above, cities retain the power to regulate carry by non-permittees in stadiums and convention centers. And carrying a firearm openly may not be done if such carry manifests any intent to intimidate another or causes alarm for the safety of others.

All Persons: Unloaded rifles and shotguns may be kept in gun racks or cases within a vehicle. Long guns are considered "loaded" only if the weapons' chambers are loaded or loaded magazines are attached to the guns. One may have loaded magazines nearby and still be lawful.

Long guns in vehicles must be unloaded regardless of one's permit status. Carry licenses only authorize loaded handgun carry. And all firearms carried in snowmobiles must be unloaded.

West Virginia

Total prohibition *(+2, preemption law strengthened, no carry bans at fairs or festivals)* **Total freedom**

0 ------- 10 ------- 20 ------- 30 ------- 40 ------- 50 ------- 60 ------- 70 ------- 80 ------ 90 ------ 100

^

CHECKLIST

***Standard firearms & ammo:** no permit required for possession or sale – see p. 3
***Semi-auto guns & high capacity magazines:** no permit required for possession or sale
***Machine guns & suppressors:** ownership lawful per federal law compliance
***Firearm law uniformity:** preemption law, localities prohibited from most regulation; but local restrictions still possible in municipally owned bldgs & recreation ctrs.
***Right of Self Defense:** NRA-model castle doctrine, *stand your ground* in public areas
***Open carry:** unrestricted under state law; some localities may regulate this independently
***Licensed concealed carry:** licenses issued on a "shall issue" basis to residents only
***Constitutional or "no permit required" concealed carry:** yes – see below
***Out-of-state permit recognition:** conditional recognition of permits from other states (see p. 65)
***Weapons allowed for *licensed* carry:** limited to handguns only

VEHICLES

***Vehicle carry by non-permittees:** loaded handguns may be carried anywhere in a vehicle by persons 21 years and older; rifles and shotguns must be unloaded and secured in cases
***Vehicle gun possession at colleges:** subject to college administrative policy
***Vehicle gun possession at K-12 schools:** West Virginia permittee w/loaded handgun lawful; permittee must be at least 21 & lock gun in secure compartment when car is unoccupied
***Duty to notify LEO of permit/carry status:** upon demand of police officer
***RV carry while "boondocking":** parking lot owners may *not* prohibit guns in vehicles – see p.8

***State Parks:** concealed handgun carry by recognized licensees permitted
***Restaurants serving alcohol:** permittees may carry while eating in dining areas – see p.3
***Hotels:** subject to hotel policy enforcement – see p.7
***Airports:** carry allowed in non-sterile terminal areas & parking lots – see p.9

West Virginia's character was exemplified during the Civil War when many of her native sons took their privately owned arms to battle, making gun ownership a deeply engrained tradition. In 2016, the state reflected this history by enacting "permitless carry" for law-abiding persons 21 years and older.

Recognized permittees: Permits to carry concealed handguns are still issued by sheriffs to residents who are at least 18 years old. Provisional licenses for 18-20 year olds remain valid until the licensee turns 21. Licenses for persons 21 and older are valid for five years. Licenses only allow the carry of handguns and are not issued to nonresidents. But agreements with other states for recognition of their permits do exist. The permittee from the recognized state must be a non-resident and at least 21 years old. Permittees may carry loaded, concealed handguns in vehicles or on foot in most public areas. Some local ordinances may restrict carry in places such as municipal buildings. Other prohibited areas are listed in the "all persons" section below.

Persons without recognized permits: Anyone who is 21 years or older, a U.S. citizen or legal resident and not a criminal may carry a concealed weapon in a vehicle or on his person in most public areas. This "permitless carry" provision includes any lawful deadly weapon, not just handguns. Military personnel under 21 may carry concealed handguns, but not other weapons, without a license.

Open carry of a firearm on foot is allowed in most public areas that are not restricted by local ordinance. Cities may still restrict open carry on municipal property by posting signs. But parking lot storage is O.K. if the weapon remains concealed from view.

All Persons: Shotguns and rifles transported in vehicles should remain unloaded for everyone, even recognized permittees. "Unloaded" means no rounds in the chambers or *attached* magazines of the weapons. Loaded, *detached* magazines are lawful for carry anywhere in the vehicle.

Along with some universally restricted areas (such as federal buildings), carry is prohibited to everyone in courthouses, schools (includes vocational schools but private K-12 may set their own rules), the state capitol and any private or city property posting signs. Permittees may keep loaded handguns in their vehicles at the state capitol and on school grounds (see checklist). And most property owners may not prohibit guns in vehicles parked on their lots if the firearms are hidden from view and the vehicles remain locked.

Wisconsin

Total prohibition *(+0, great improvements, some minor tweaking required)* **Total freedom**

0 ------- 10 ------- 20 ------- 30 ------- 40 ------- 50 ------- 60 ------- 70 ------- 80 ------ 90 ------ 100

^ (between 80 and 90)

CHECKLIST

***Standard firearms & ammo:** no permit required for possession or sale – see p. 3
***Semi-auto guns & high capacity magazines:** no permit required for possession or sale
***Machine guns & suppressors:** machine guns require approval of sheriff and federal law compliance; suppressor ownership lawful w/federal law compliance
***Firearm law uniformity:** preemption statute, firearm laws uniform throughout state
***Right of Self-Defense:** NRA-model castle doctrine, *stand your ground* in vehicle only
***Open carry:** unrestricted under state law and affirmed by statute and A.G. opinion
***Licensed concealed carry:** licenses issued on a "shall issue" basis to residents only
***Constitutional or "no permit required" concealed carry:** no
***Out-of-state permit recognition:** conditional recognition of permits from other states (see p. 65)
***Weapons allowed for *licensed* carry:** limited to handguns, stun guns and billy clubs

VEHICLES

***Vehicle carry by non-permittees:** handguns may be loaded; long guns must be unloaded; no firearms may be concealed (see below)
***Vehicle gun possession at colleges:** lawful for any gun owner (permittee or non-permittee)
***Vehicle gun possession at K-12 schools:** Wisconsin permittee must unload & encase gun
***Duty to notify LEO of permit status:** upon demand of police officer
***RV carry while "boondocking":** parking lot owners may *not* prohibit guns in vehicles – see p.8

***State Parks:** concealed handgun carry by recognized licensees permitted
***Restaurants serving alcohol:** permittees may carry while eating in dining areas – see p.3
***Hotels:** subject to hotel policy enforcement & "force of law" posting prohibitions – see p.7
***Airports:** carry allowed in non-sterile terminal areas unless posted; car carry in parking lots O.K.

Sportsmen visiting Wisconsin will enjoy the numerous wildlife areas set aside for hunting and fishing activities while tourists will find the temperate climate quite refreshing. With the 2011 passage of its concealed carry law, Wisconsin has become a much more inviting place for gun owners.

Recognized permittees: Wisconsin requires a license issued by the state's Department of Justice to carry a concealed, loaded handgun. Such licenses are valid for five years and are only issued to Wisconsin residents who are at least 21 years old. Wisconsin will recognize carry permits from states that perform background checks on their licensees as long as the licensee is 21 years or older, not a Wisconsin resident and has a photo ID. A permittee may carry a handgun, either openly or concealed, in most public areas except law enforcement offices, mental health facilities, courthouses, K-12 schools and secure areas (marked by signage or security screenings). Colleges, local governments, special event promoters and most private businesses may post signs against carry within their buildings. But vehicles parked on their lots, and residential dwellings at colleges, are exempt from these prohibitions. And employers may not ban guns in permittee-employee cars.

Persons without recognized permits: Loaded handguns may not be concealed in any motor vehicle (includes ATVs and boats). Wisconsin courts have developed a strict definition of what constitutes "concealed." Even having a gun on your front seat is prohibited. So, despite amending its law to allow handguns to be uncased and loaded, Wisconsin continues to restrict "open carry" in vehicles through a restrictive definition of "concealed." Non-permittees with loaded handguns should keep the weapons stowed in the trunk or rear storage area where they are not within anyone's immediate reach.

Open carry on foot is allowed in most public areas as long as the handgun is in a visible belt holster. Wisconsin affirmed the right of open carry by statute. Police are now prohibited from using disorderly conduct ordinances to arrest someone who is openly carrying a handgun.

All Persons: Long guns in a vehicle must be unloaded in both the chamber and magazine. But loaded, unattached magazines may be kept anywhere in the vehicle. This applies to both licensees and non-licensees since Wisconsin's carry law does not affect the possession of long guns.

Most parking lots are O.K. for firearm carry as long as the gun remains secured in one's vehicle. Property owners' right to prohibit carry only extends to buildings and not parking facilities.

Wyoming

Total prohibition ***(+0, the "cowboy state" lives up to its name when it comes to guns)*** **Total freedom**

0 ------- 10 ------- 20 ------- 30 ------- 40 ------- 50 ------- 60 ------- 70 ------- 80 ------ 90 ------ 100

^

CHECKLIST

- ***Standard firearms & ammo:** no permit required for possession or sale – see p.3
- ***Semi-auto guns & high capacity magazines:** no permit required for possession or sale
- ***Machine guns & suppressors:** ownership lawful per federal law compliance
- ***Firearm law uniformity:** preemption law, firearm laws uniform throughout the state
- ***Right of Self-Defense:** NRA-model castle doctrine, *stand your ground* in public areas
- ***Open carry:** unrestricted in most public areas and generally accepted
- ***Licensed concealed carry:** licenses issued on a "shall issue" basis to residents only
- ***Constitutional or "no permit required" concealed carry:** limited – see below
- ***Out-of-state permit recognition:** conditional recognition of permits from other states (see p. 65)
- ***Weapons allowed for *licensed* carry:** limited to handguns only

VEHICLES

- ***Vehicle carry by non-permittees:** non-residents may carry loaded firearms in plain view or secured in gun cases anywhere in the vehicle; residents who are 21 years or older may carry loaded firearms openly or concealed anywhere in the vehicle
- ***Vehicle gun possession at colleges:** subject to college administrative policy
- ***Vehicle gun possession at K-12 schools:** Wyoming permittee w/loaded handgun lawful
- ***Duty to notify LEO of permit/carry status:** upon demand of police officer
- ***RV carry while "boondocking":** parking lot owners may restrict gun carry by visitors – see p.8

- ***State Parks:** concealed handgun carry by recognized licensees permitted
- ***Restaurants serving alcohol:** permittees may carry while eating in dining areas – see p.3
- ***Hotels:** subject to hotel policy enforcement & "force of law" posting prohibitions – see p.7
- ***Airports:** carry allowed in non-sterile terminal areas & parking lots – see p. 9

The "Cowboy State's" reputation as "gun-friendly" territory was buttressed by its 2011 adoption of constitutional or "no permit required" concealed carry. Although Wyoming limits this right to residents only, the law is a good indication of the state's classic attitude on firearm rights.

Recognized permittees: Wyoming issues licenses to carry loaded handguns concealed on the person. These permits are issued by the Attorney General through the sheriff of an applicant's home county for five-year terms to qualified residents 21 years or older. The state does not grant permits to nonresidents but will recognize permits from other states so long as they recognize Wyoming permits and issue licenses through a state agency. Recognized permittees may carry concealed handguns in most public places except athletic events, school facilities (including colleges and universities), bars, courthouses, legislative meetings and the state capitol.

Persons without recognized permits: A non-resident may carry a loaded handgun in a vehicle if the weapon is in plain view. This would include handguns in visible belt holsters or displayed on the vehicle's dashboard or passenger seat. Wyoming only prohibits the "wearing or carrying" of a concealed weapon. So a handgun not worn or carried by the person may be secured in a commercial gun case, glove compartment, or other closed container.

A non-resident may also openly carry a handgun while on foot. The weapon must be visible to casual observation and should be secured in a snapped belt holster. Wyoming's preemption law prevents localities from regulating any aspect of this carry mode.

Any person who has been a resident of Wyoming for at least six months, is 21 years or older and has no disqualifying criminal past may carry a concealed firearm without a permit. He is still under the same carry restrictions as permittees. But his concealed carry requires no permit.

All Persons: Non-residents may transport loaded long guns in gun racks or commercial gun cases. Because Wyoming only authorizes concealed *handgun* carry with a license, long guns may not be concealed on the person even if one possesses a recognized permit. But Wyoming residents who fit the above qualifications may transport long guns anywhere in a vehicle.

Travel to Canada and Mexico

Despite a common language and a somewhat similar heritage, Canada's legal treatment of firearms is a shocking reminder of just how different America's neighbor to the North remains. Canada prohibits the importation of any handgun without an Authorization to Transport (ATT). These ATTs are rarely issued to Americans and are given to Canadians on a highly discretionary basis. Travelers without an ATT who attempt to enter Canada with handguns will have their weapons confiscated, their vehicles impounded and could face prosecution. Securely casing the handgun and stowing it in the trunk will not prevent seizure. Mere possession of a handgun anywhere in a vehicle without an ATT is illegal.

Most semi-automatic military pattern firearms are also prohibited from importation. The Canadian parliament enacted a series of draconian gun laws that effectively ban almost every weapon that looks even remotely military. And in 2020 this ban was extended to include AR-15s and other military-pattern rifles that were not directly affected by the initial law. M1 Garands are still exempt from this general prohibition and treated like standard sporting rifles. But the importation of most military pattern weapons as well as any Class III firearms (machine guns, short barreled rifles and short barreled shotguns) is strictly prohibited. And over 5 shot magazines for center-fire long guns as well as over 10 shot magazines for center-fire pistols are banned from entering the country.

Most individuals may only bring those rifles and shotguns classified as "sporting" into the country. Sporting weapons are defined as "regular sporting rifles or shotguns with barrels over 18.5 inches and longer than 26 inches in overall length." A Non-Resident Firearms Declaration Form is now required for importation. Such forms must be completed in triplicate before a traveler reaches the Canadian border but should not be signed until arriving at the port of entry. These permits cost $25.00 and are valid for 60 days. Travelers should contact Canadian authorities at **1-800-731-4000, www.rcmp.gc.ca, Royal Canadian Mounted Police, Canadian Firearms Program, Ottawa, Ontario K1A 0R2** to receive copies of these forms.

Upon reaching the border, you should have your firearm unloaded and separate from any ammunition. The weapon should also be in a gun case that is hidden from view or stowed in the trunk. A secure locking device, such as a trigger or cable lock, must be in place so the weapon cannot be fired. And, if left unattended, the vehicle must be locked. If asked by Customs for a reason why you are transporting a firearm into the country, the traveler should respond that he intends to engage in hunting or officially-sanctioned target competition. Personal defense is not a reason for firearm possession in Canada.

Upon returning to the U.S., you should have proof that the firearms you took into Canada are yours and that you are not importing new firearms into the country. Customs officials recommend a purchase receipt, bill of sale, household inventory list, packing list or a Customs Form 4457 completed prior to your trip. Some customs officials will also accept the Canadian "firearms declaration form" as proof that you owned the gun prior to entering Canada.

Travel to Mexico with firearms is not recommended. Possession of most firearms as well as ammunition is illegal. As Marine Sgt. Andrew Tahmooressi found to his horror, travelers who visit Mexico with firearms are arrested and forced to languish in prison until the intervention of U.S. authorities secures their release. Mexican law presumes your guilt. In other words, once you are arrested, you are guilty until proven innocent. Special permits may be obtained to bring hunting rifles into the country. Contact the Mexican consulate for information at **(202) 736-1000.**

Contact Agencies

Attorney General of Alabama
501 Washington Ave.
Montgomery, AL 36104
(334) 242-7300
www.ago.alabama.gov

Alaskan State Police
5700 E. Tudor Road
Anchorage, AK 99507
(907) 269-0392
www.dps.alaska.gov

Arizona Dept. of Public Safety
P.O. Box 6488
Phoenix, AZ 85005
(602) 256-6280
www.azdps.gov

Arkansas State Police HQ
1 State Police Plaza Drive
Little Rock, AR 72209
(501) 618-8000
www.asp.state.ar.us

California Bureau of Firearms
P.O. Box 820200
Sacramento, California 94203
(916) 210-2300
www.oag.ca.gov

Colorado Bureau of Investigation
690 Kipling St. – Ste. #3000
Lakewood, CO 80215
(303) 813-5700
www.colorado.gov/cbi

Connecticut Dept. / Public Safety
1111 Country Club Road
Middletown, CT 06457
(860) 685-8290
www.ct.gov/despp

Attorney General of Delaware
820 North French Street
Wilmington, DE 19801
(302) 577-8500
www.attorneygeneral.delaware.gov

Washington Metro Police
300 Indiana Ave. NW – 5th Floor
Washington D.C. 20001
(202) 727-4275
www.mpdc.dc.gov

Florida Division of Licenses
P.O. Box 6687
Tallahassee, FL 32314 6687
(850) 245-5691
www.freshfromflorida.com

Attorney General of Georgia
40 Capitol Square SW
Atlanta, GA 30334
(404) 458-3600
www.law.ga.gov

Attorney General of Hawaii
425 Queen Street
Honolulu, HI 96813
(808) 586-1500
www.ag.hawaii.gov

Attorney General of Idaho
P.O. Box 83720
Boise, ID 83720
(208) 334-2400
www.ag.idaho.gov

Illinois State Police
801 S. 7th St. - #400-M
Springfield, IL 62703
(217) 782-7980
www.isp.state.il.us/

Indiana State Police
100 N. Senate Ave. / N302
Indianapolis, IN 46204
(317) 232-8264
www.in.gov/isp

Iowa Dept. of Public Safety
215 East 7th Street, 4th FL.
Des Moines, IA 50319
(515) 725-6230
www.dps.state.ia.us

Attorney General of Kansas
120 SW 10th Ave. – 2nd Floor
Topeka, KS 66612
(785) 291-3765
www.ag.ks.gov

Kentucky State Police
919 Versailles Rd.
Frankfort, KY 40601
(502) 782-1800 or 227-8700
www.Kentuckystatepolice.org

Louisiana State Police / CHP
P.O. Box 66375
Baton Rouge, LA 70896
(225) 925-4867
www.lsp.org

Maine Dept. of Public Safety
45 Commerce / State House 164
Augusta, ME 04333
(207) 624-7210
www.maine.gov/dps

Maryland State Police
1111 Reisterstown Rd.
Pikesville, MD 21208
(410) 653-4500
www.mdsp.maryland.gov

Firearms Bureau / Mass.
200 Arlington St. – Suite 2200
Chelsea, MA 02150
(617) 660-4782
www.mass.gov/eopss

Michigan State Police
P.O. Box 30634
Lansing, MI 48909
(517) 284-3700
www.michigan.gov/msp

Minnesota Dept. of Public Safety
445 Minnesota St.
St. Paul, MN 55101
(651) 201-7000
www.dps.mn.gov

Mississippi Hwy. Patrol
P.O. Box 958
Jackson, MS 39205-0958
(601) 987-1212
www.dps.state.ms.us

Attorney General of Missouri
207 West High St., P.O. Box 899
Jefferson City, MO 65102
(573) 751-3321
www.ago.mo.gov

Attorney General of Montana
215 N. Sanders / P.O. Box 201401
Helena, MT 59620 1401
(406) 444-2026
www.dojmt.gov

Nebraska State Police
1600 Highway 2
Lincoln, NE 68502
(402) 471-4545
www.statepatrol.nebraska.gov

Nevada Dept. of Public Safety
555 Wright Way
Carson City, NV 89711-0900
(775) 684-4808
www.dps.nv.gov

New Hampshire State Police
33 Hazen Drive – Room 106
Concord, NH 03305
(603) 223-3873
www.nh.gov/safety

New Jersey State Police
P.O. Box 7068
W. Trenton, NJ 08628
(609) 882-2000
www.njsp.org

New Mexico Dept. of Public Safety
6301 Indian School Rd. NE - #310
Albuquerque, NM 87110
(505) 841-8053
www.dps.state.nm.us

New York State Police
1220 Washington Ave. Bldg. 22
Albany, NY 12226
(518) 783-3211
www.troopers.ny.gov

North Carolina A.G.
9001 Mail Service Center
Raleigh, NC 27699-9001
(919) 716-6400
www.ncdoj.gov

North Dakota Attorney General
600 E. Blvd. Avenue / Dept. 125
Bismarck, ND 58505
(701) 328-2210
www.attorneygeneral.nd.gov

Ohio Attorney General
30 East Broad St. – 14th Floor
Columbus, OH 43215 3428
(800) 282-0515
www.ohioattorneygeneral.gov

Oklahoma B of I
6600 N. Harvey
Oklahoma City, OK 73116
(405) 879-2690
www.ok.gov/osbi

Oregon Attorney General
1162 Court St. NE
Salem, OR 97301
(503) 378-4400
www.doj.state.or.us

Pennsylvania Attorney General
16th Floor / Strawberry Square
Harrisburg, PA 17120
(717) 787-3391
www.attorneygeneral.gov

Rhode Island A. G.
150 S. Main St.
Providence, RI 02903
(401) 274-4400
www.riag.ri.gov

South Carolina (SLED)
P.O. Box 21398
Columbia, SC 29221
(803) 896-7015
www.sled.sc.gov

South Dakota Secretary of State
500 E. Capitol Ave. – Suite 204
Pierre, SD 57501 5070
(605) 773-3537
www.sdsos.gov

Tennessee DPS
P.O. Box 945
Nashville, TN 37202
(615) 251-8590
www.tn.gov/safety

Texas Dept. of Public Safety
P.O. Box 4087
Austin, TX 78773
(512) 424-7293
www.dps.texas.gov

Utah Dept. of Public Safety
3888 West 5400 South
Taylorsville, UT 84129
(801) 965-4445
www.publicsafety.utah.gov

Vermont State Police
45 State Drive
Waterbury, VT 05671
(802) 244-8727
www.vsp.vermont.gov

Virginia State Police
P.O. Box 27472
Richmond, VA 23261 7472
(804) 674-2000
www.vsp.state.va.us

Washington Attorney General
P.O. Box 40100
Olympia, WA 98504
(360) 753-6200
www.atg.wa.gov

West Virginia A.G.
Capitol Bldg. 1, #26E
Charleston, WV 25305
(304) 558-2021
www.ago.wv.gov

Wisconsin Attorney General
P.O. Box 7857
Madison, WI 53703
(608) 266-1221
www.doj.state.wi.us

Wyoming Attorney General
208 S. College Drive
Cheyenne, WY 82002
(307) 777-7181
http://ag.wyo.gov

Reciprocity, Recognition & Permitless Carry

Constitutional or "Permitless Carry" States

Alaska, Arizona, Arkansas, Idaho, Kentucky, Kansas, Maine, Mississippi, Missouri, Montana (limited – see p. 37), **New Hampshire, North Dakota** (residents only), **Oklahoma, South Dakota, Vermont, West Virginia** and **Wyoming** (residents only) allow "on foot" concealed carry without a permit. (for limits – see text).

Automatic Recognition States

Alabama, Arizona, Arkansas, Alaska, Idaho, Indiana, Iowa, Kansas, Kentucky, Michigan*, Mississippi, Missouri, North Carolina, Ohio, Oklahoma, South Dakota, Tennessee, Utah, Virginia** recognize all other states but may limit recognition to certain residency requirements as noted by (*) or (**) or (_). (see bottom of page)

Conditional Recognition / Reciprocity States

The states listed below recognize other states on a state-by-state basis. Interpretations of reciprocity statutes by state administrators are the basis for this list. As always, any bureaucratic decision is subject to change. Travelers should verify the status of their permits by visiting www.gunlawguide.com or using the state contacts on pages 63 & 64. The list below is based on information received from the various state agencies on December 1, 2020. **States not listed below or in the automatic recognition or constitutional carry paragraphs above do not recognize any out-of-state permits.**

Colorado* *recognizes permits from* Alabama, Alaska, Arizona, Arkansas, Delaware, Florida, Georgia, Idaho, Indiana, Iowa, Kansas, Kentucky, Louisiana, Michigan, Mississippi, Missouri, Montana, Nebraska, New Hampshire, New Mexico, North Carolina, North Dakota, Ohio, Oklahoma, Pennsylvania, South Dakota, Tennessee, Texas, Utah, Virginia, West Virginia, Wisconsin, Wyoming ***(must be 21 or older)***

Update at www.gunlawguide.com

Delaware *recognizes permits from* Alaska, Arizona, Arkansas, Colorado, Florida, Idaho (enhanced permit) Kansas, Kentucky, Maine, Michigan, Missouri, New Mexico, North Carolina, North Dakota, Ohio, Oklahoma, South Dakota (enhanced permits), Tennessee, Texas, Utah, West Virginia

Update at www.gunlawguide.com

Florida* *recognizes permits from* Alabama, Alaska, Arizona, Arkansas, Colorado, Delaware, Georgia, Idaho, Indiana, Iowa, Kansas, Kentucky, Louisiana, Maine, Michigan, Mississippi, Missouri, Montana, Nebraska, Nevada, New Hampshire, New Mexico, North Carolina, North Dakota, Ohio, Oklahoma, Pennsylvania, South Carolina, South Dakota, Tennessee, Texas, Utah, Virginia, West Virginia, Wyoming ***(must be 21 or older)***

Update at www.gunlawguide.com

Georgia *recognizes permits from* Alabama, Alaska, Arizona, Arkansas, Colorado, Florida, Idaho, Indiana, Iowa, Kansas, Kentucky, Louisiana, Maine, Michigan, Mississippi, Missouri, Montana, New Hampshire, North Carolina, North Dakota, Ohio, Oklahoma, Pennsylvania, South Carolina, South Dakota, Tennessee, Texas, Utah, Virginia, West Virginia, Wisconsin, Wyoming

Update at www.gunlawguide.com

Louisiana *recognizes permits from* Alabama, Alaska, Arizona, Arkansas, Colorado, Florida, Georgia, Idaho, Indiana, Iowa, Kansas, Kentucky, Maine, Michigan, Minnesota, Mississippi, Missouri, Montana, Nebraska, Nevada, New Hampshire, North Carolina, North Dakota, Ohio, Oklahoma, Pennsylvania, South Carolina, South Dakota, Tennessee, Texas, Utah, Virginia, Washington, West Virginia, Wisconsin, Wyoming ***(must be 21 or older)***

Update at www.gunlawguide.com

***States with this star only recognize permittees who are residents of the state where the permit was issued.**
States that are UNDERLINED will not recognize out-of-state permits held by their residents.
****Ohio recognizes some, but not all, out-of-state permits held by Ohio residents – see p. 46**
North Dakota issues Class 1 and Class 2 licenses. This list encompasses Class 1 licenses only.

State	Recognizes permits from
Maine* *recognizes permits from* ***Update at*** www.gunlawguide.com	Alabama, Alaska, Arizona, Delaware, Florida, Georgia, Idaho, Iowa, Kansas, Kentucky, Louisiana, Michigan, Mississippi, Missouri, Nebraska, New Hampshire, North Carolina, North Dakota, Ohio, Oklahoma, Utah, Virginia, Wyoming
Minnesota *recognizes permits from* ***Update at*** www.gunlawguide.com	Alaska, Delaware, Idaho (enhanced permits), Illinois, Kansas, Kentucky, Louisiana, Michigan, New Jersey, New Mexico, North Dakota, Rhode Island, South Carolina, South Dakota (enhanced permits), West Virginia ***(must be 21 or older)***
Montana *recognizes permits from* ***Update at*** www.gunlawguide.com	**ALL STATES** that issue permits **EXCEPT** Delaware, Hawaii, Maine, New Hampshire, Rhode Island, District of Columbia
Nebraska *recognizes permits from* ***Update at*** www.gunlawguide.com	**ALL STATES** that issue permits **EXCEPT** Alabama, Delaware, Georgia, Idaho (regular permit), Indiana, Maryland, Massachusetts, Mississippi, New Hampshire, New Jersey, New York, Pennsylvania, Rhode Island, Washington, South Dakota (regular permit) ***(21 or older)***
Nevada *recognizes permits from* ***Update at*** www.gunlawguide.com	Alaska, Arizona, Arkansas, Florida, Idaho (enhanced permits), Illinois, Kansas, Kentucky, Louisiana, Massachusetts, Michigan, Minnesota, Mississippi (enhanced permits), Montana, New Mexico, North Dakota, Ohio, Oklahoma, South Dakota (enhanced permits), South Carolina, Tennessee, Texas, Utah, Virginia, West Virginia, Wisconsin, Wyoming
New Hampshire *recog. permits from* ***Update at*** www.gunlawguide.com	Alabama, Alaska, Arizona, Arkansas, Colorado, Florida, Georgia, Idaho, Indiana, Iowa, Kansas, Kentucky, Louisiana, Maine, Michigan, Missouri, Mississippi, North Carolina, North Dakota, Ohio, Oklahoma, Wyoming, Pennsylvania, South Dakota, Tennessee, Utah, Virginia, West Virginia,
New Mexico *recognizes permit from* ***Update at*** www.gunlawguide.com	Alaska, Arizona, Arkansas, Colorado, Delaware, Idaho (enhanced permits), Florida, Kansas, Michigan, Mississippi, Missouri, Nebraska, Nevada, North Carolina, North Dakota, Ohio, Oklahoma, South Carolina, Tennessee, Texas, Virginia, West Virginia, Wyoming ***(21 or older)***
North Dakota *recognizes permits from* ***Update at*** www.gunlawguide.com	Alabama, Alaska, Arizona, Arkansas, Colorado, Delaware, Florida, Georgia, Idaho, Indiana, Iowa, Kansas, Kentucky, Louisiana, Maine, Michigan, Minnesota, Mississippi, Missouri, Montana, Nebraska, Nevada, New Hampshire, New Mexico, North Carolina, Ohio, Oklahoma, Pennsylvania, South Carolina, South Dakota, Tennessee, Texas, Utah, Virginia, Washington, West Virginia, Wisconsin, Wyoming
Pennsylvania* *recognizes permits from* ***Update at*** www.gunlawguide.com	Alabama, Alaska, Arizona, Arkansas, Colorado, Florida, Georgia, Idaho (enhanced permits), Indiana, Iowa, Kansas, Kentucky, Louisiana, Michigan, Mississippi, Missouri, Montana, New Hampshire, North Carolina, North Dakota, Ohio, Oklahoma, South Dakota, Tennessee, Texas, Utah (excludes provisional permits), West Virginia (regular permits), Wisconsin, Wyoming ***(must be 21 or older)***

***States with this star only recognize permittees who are residents of the state where the permit was issued.**
States that are UNDERLINED will not recognize out-of-state permits held by their residents.
****Ohio recognizes some, but not all, out-of-state permits held by Ohio residents – see p. 46**
North Dakota issues Class 1 and Class 2 licenses. This list encompasses Class 1 licenses only.

South Carolina* *recog. permits from*

Update at www.gunlawguide.com

Alaska, Arizona, Arkansas, Florida, Georgia, Idaho (enhanced permits), Hawaii, Kansas, Kentucky, Louisiana, Michigan, Minnesota, Mississippi (enhanced permits), Missouri, Nebraska, New Mexico, North Carolina, North Dakota, Ohio, Oklahoma, Rhode Island, South Dakota (enhanced permits), Texas, Tennessee, Virginia, West Virginia, Wyoming ***(must be 21 or older)***

Texas *recognizes permits from*

Update at www.gunlawguide.com

ALL STATES that issue permits **EXCEPT** D.C, Maine, Minnesota, New Hampshire, Oregon, Rhode Island (local issued permits, AG. Permits O.K.), Wisconsin ***(must be 21 or older)***

Washington *recognizes permits from*

Update at www.gunlawguide.com

Idaho (enhanced permits only), Kansas, Louisiana, Michigan, North Carolina, North Dakota, Ohio, Oklahoma, South Dakota (enhanced permittees who are 21 years or older), Utah ***(must be 21 or older)***

West Virginia *recognizes permits from*

Update at www.gunlawguide.com

Alabama, Alaska, Arizona, Arkansas, Colorado, Delaware, Florida, Georgia, Idaho, Indiana, Iowa, Kansas, Kentucky, Louisiana, Michigan, Mississippi, Missouri, Montana, Nebraska, Nevada, New Hampshire, New Mexico, North Carolina, North Dakota, Ohio, Oklahoma, Pennsylvania, South Carolina, South Dakota, Tennessee, Texas, Utah, Virginia, Wisconsin, Wyoming ***(must be 21 or older)***

Wisconsin *recognizes permit from*

Update at www.gunlawguide.com

Alabama, Alaska, Arizona, Arkansas, California, Colorado, Connecticut, Delaware, District of Columbia, Florida (permits issued to non-residents only), Georgia, Hawaii, Idaho, Illinois, Indiana, Iowa, Kansas, Kentucky, Louisiana (permits issued on or after 3/9/15), Maryland, Massachusetts (Class A), Michigan, Minnesota, Mississippi, Montana, Missouri (only permits issued after 8/28/13; no provisional licenses), Nebraska, Nevada, New Mexico, New York, North Carolina, North Dakota, Ohio, Oklahoma (permits issued on or after 10/1/18), Pennsylvania, Rhode Island, South Carolina, South Dakota (enhanced & Gold permits) Tennessee, Texas, Utah, Virginia (non-resident permits only), Washington, West Virginia (no provisional licenses), Wyoming, Puerto Rico, U.S. Virgin Islands ***(must be 21 or older)***

Wyoming *recognizes permits from*

Update at www.gunlawguide.com

Alabama, Alaska, Arizona, Arkansas, Colorado, Florida, Georgia, Idaho, Indiana, Iowa, Kansas, Kentucky, Louisiana, Maine, Michigan, Mississippi, Missouri, Montana, Nebraska, Nevada, New Hampshire, New Mexico, North Carolina, North Dakota, Ohio, Oklahoma, Pennsylvania, South Carolina, South Dakota, Tennessee, Texas, Utah, Virginia, West Virginia, Wisconsin

These lists are taken from official sources at time of printing and may be subject to bureaucratic error by the state agency administering the list. Check www.gunlawguide.com for updates throughout the year.

- and -

This list encompasses "regular" permits for the states covered unless otherwise noted. Coverage for Tennessee permits only includes the "enhanced" licenses and not the "concealed carry only" licenses.

***States with this star only recognize permittees who are residents of the state where the permit was issued.**
States that are UNDERLINED will not recognize out-of-state permits held by their residents.
****Ohio recognizes some, but not all, out-of-state permits held by Ohio residents – see p. 46**
North Dakota issues Class 1 and Class 2 licenses. This list encompasses Class 1 licenses only.